Churches in Crisis

Churches in Crisis

by

Lloyd M. Perry
and
Gilbert A. Peterson

MOODY PRESS
CHICAGO

Library of Congress Cataloging in Publication Data

Perry, Lloyd Merle.
  Churches in crisis.

  Bibliography: p.
  1. Church consultation—Case studies
2. Church controversies—Case studies. I. Peter-
son, Gilbert, 1935-   . II. Title
BV652.35.P47   254   81-38427
ISBN 0-8024-1551-2   AACR2

Contents

The case studies presented in this book are from actual churches in which the authors have had a consulting ministry. Names, dates, and some details have been altered to protect the identity of those churches.

Foreword

"Church consultation" is perhaps a new term to some church workers, but it is certainly not a new concept. When the apostle Paul sent Timothy to Corinth, and left Titus in Crete, he was engaging them in the ministry of church consultation. There were problems to solve, leaders to train, goals to reach, and spiritual needs to be met.

Some denominations have "built-in consultation" available in the person of superintendents and bishops. We assume that those overseers are experienced in the consultation ministry, but, alas, sometimes they are not. This book ought to be of great value to them as they help local pastors and churches face and solve their problems.

Many churches, of course, are independent in their ministry. To whom do they turn when there is a crisis in the church? Too often, the "solution" is either a church split or a resignation, and often both. If both pastors and lay church leaders understood and applied the principles outlined in this book, we would have fewer church splits and fewer pastors looking for new ministries or (even worse) forsaking the ministry of the Word for secular employment.

But this book is valuable not only in helping us *solve* local church problems. It is equally as valuable in helping us to *avoid* those problems. Blessed is that congregation whose spiritual leadership can discern the spirits and know when problems are about to appear! There is a family resemblance to most church problems, and this book helps us to recognize them. Prevention is always better than cure.

The authors are experienced in this field and have done us a great service in sharing their experience with us. This book is pioneering new territory for most of us, but it is territory that we must claim and conquer. If secular organizations can have their expert "trouble-shooters" to help them detect, define, and solve problems, then surely the church can have its "consultants" for the same purposes. I have every reason to believe that the proper use of the principles outlined in these pages will help any pastor or lay leader become a part of the answer instead of a part of the problem.

WARREN W. WIERSBE

1

The Church in Today's World

Change is one of the primary identification marks of our society and culture. However, it is not the fact of change that poses the greatest threat—it is the speed of change. We no longer have the luxury of adapting gradually to major changes in our lives. We must flex, bend, and cope with a myriad of social, ethical, political, educational, physical, technical, and scientific changes that constantly bombard us. Tension, stress, and physchological dysfunction are common in our society.

There are a number of significant characteristics that now mark us as a people and as a nation. Although the following are not to be considered the only factors affecting us, they are major influences upon us as individuals, families, and churches.

We have become hermits in the midst of a mob. Apartment complexes and condominiums with extensive security systems are illustrations of how we can isolate ourselves in the midst of groups of people. That isolation can in turn, produce loneliness. In 1940, 60 percent of the US population lived in towns under 40,000 in population. A small town atmosphere was in evidence. Today 20 percent of the population lives there. Although cities have been with us for over five thousand years, the concept of a megalopolis, or urban concentration, is only thirty years old. In that context, the suburbs now join with the city as sites for homes and jobs, and the city atmosphere is expanded.

We have become pawns of the powerful. We have become a nation of people whose lives are governed by a few. Decision-making is more a national practice than a local or individual one. We have national television, newspapers, and periodicals. Even ethical and moral decisions in many cases have been prescribed by a minority.

We are speed conscious. Today man can travel at a rate exceeding 24,000 miles per hour, and the end is not yet in sight. Just a few years ago top speed was 800 miles per hour. One hundred fifty years ago man traveled at the amazing rate of 20 miles per hour with a pair of strong horses and a well-oiled carriage. In slightly more than two lifetimes man has doubled his speed of travel eight times.

Man has also become a collector and disseminator of knowledge. It is reported that in the 1500s, Europe produced approximately 1000 copies per year. In the US in 1950 there were 11,000 *titles* produced. By 1960 it had increased to 15,000, and by 1980 the number was over 33,000 titles, with hundreds of millions of individual copies. And that is only one medium. Data gathering by orbiting satellites boggles the mind. It has been estimated that less than 5 percent of the data can be filtered and utilized. We know more than ever before and are overwhelmed by it.

We are a nation of nomads. Thirty percent of the American public moves its place of residence every year. The extended family keeps in contact by telephone or tape recorder if it maintains contact at all.

We are in a service-oriented economy. Those that work in the serving professions, such as education, medicine, or governmental agencies, numerically far exceed those who work in the production of hard goods.

We are leveling off in population growth, which affects our future economy. It means that when the large population bubble that has been going through our society finally reaches retirement, it will have to be supported by a much smaller group of income-producing workers.

New sources for energy, as well as new shortages, are before us. Communication will replace transportation. It has been suggested that a video-computer terminal in the homes of employees will replace the office building, parking lots, and car pools. If that comes to pass, it cannot but help increase both the isolation of individuals and the control by the few and powerful.

Scientific developments stagger us—such things as laser communication, holography, cloning, test tube babies, chemical and electronic developments, transplants of vital organs, biofeedback, and the all-encompassing computer, which learns, remembers, sees, reasons, walks, talks, plays, gets irritable, adapts to environment, and plans its own improvements. It is not a Star Wars or Galactica imagination for entertainment purposes. Those developments are with us now—some in advanced stages.

In the context of such a culture and society is the church. The church of Jesus Christ is the actual and spiritual fellowship of all who have been regenerated by personal faith in Jesus Christ. As Ted Ward has written, "It is more than an organization; the church is *supra-organization* in that it exists above and beyond the ordinary man-made social entities and enterprises" (*The Influence of Secular Institutions on Today's Family* [St. Louis: Family '76, 1975], p. 5).

The church serves as a primary instrument in the plan of God for the spiritual nurture of families and individuals. It shall endure until He comes to receive it to Himself at the end of the age. Its form and pattern are affected by its historical setting and cultural interactions, but its purpose is established in Scripture.

Today we find a variety of ministry styles within evangelical churches, each one arising out of a combination of theological, philosophical, and cultural factors. The traditional ministry usually is identified as having an easily recognized organizational structure and set of beliefs and practices that are inherited from the past. It purports to strive for both the evangelization of the unbeliever and education of the believer.

A second church ministry style is known as aggressive, generally identifying churches who devote a considerable amount of their effort toward the course of evangelism. The program is highly structured, the leadership strong and visible, and numerical growth considered a primary indicator of success.

The third style is usually identified as renewal, emphasizing the organic life of the church and the maturing of the believer. A more informal approach is used for worship; shared leadership and a strong family emphasis are usually present.

Of course there are combinations of each of those and a broad continuum in each specific style. A particular problem that does arise is the tendency of one church to attempt to adopt another church's style or program without seriously studying the situation, principles involved, and consequences.

Churches today are also facing a fluctuation in attendance that appears to be tied to specific needs. Churches that are growing seem to be either authoritative churches, which meet the individual and family need for stability and direction in an age of chaos and constant change, or else the relational church, which meets the individual and family need for care and love in an age of fragmentation and loneliness.

One very disturbing trend in many of the growing churches is the increasing number of "spectator" Christians. They attend the morning service but nothing else. Many of the larger, growing churches are finding a widening gap developing between the Sunday morning attendance in church and the Sunday school attendance or attendance at other functions in which personal involvement is expected. Thirty years ago that was symptomatic of liberal churches, but today conservative churches are blighted with the same problem.

In the area of finance there is an increasing crisis situation developing. The church is a cash-based organization that is attempting to survive in a cashless society. Plastic money is the order of the day, but the church still depends on the offering plate. Governmental pressure and the issue of removing tax exempt status for churches is already being talked about in the highest echelons of government.

While the number of individuals going to the mission field has increased slightly, the career missionary numbers are dropping drastically, with short term missionaries providing the buffer.

More churches today have multiple staffs to help meet the increasing specialized needs of congregations. There are also serious multiple staff problems of role confusion and conflict, and those are not limited to any geographic or denominational area. In addition, a concern for family ministry without a strategy and often without cooperation is apparent. Families are often too confused to know what they need or want. The occasional sermon on "The Family" does not meet the need. In fact, it often does little more than raise the guilt level of an already guilt-laden parent.

Today's average evangelical church member has a low view of the church and what it can do for him. He feels the same way toward the church leadership. Our people are warmly evangelical when it comes to personal attitudes, but immature theologically.

Printed materials for Christian growth, doctrinal truth, and biblical exposition abound on every side. Audiovisuals, a variety of methods, and some of the finest facilities ever imagined are available. Retreats, seminars, clinics, evening courses, home studies, video tape, filmstrips, and cassette recordings offer increased learning opportunties. More are being produced daily.

The church has become number-, technique-, and program-minded. Carnal and secular values have become the rule rather than the exception. We have been measuring success by the secular standards of physical acquisitions, size, and acceptance by our contemporary society. We have even gone to the Scriptures as proof texts for our positions. That is not to suggest that puny is pure and big is bad. It does mean, however, that the church must concentrate on its reason for existence and bring every concept, technique, and program under the careful scrutiny of the complete Scriptures.

First it should be noted that our present society and culture do not provide supports for either the church or the home. We cannot look to business, education, government, the world of sports and entertainment, or any other part of our culture to provide us with help or models in our Christian life and growth process.

Second, it is also true that unless we develop a biblical philosophy of ministry, a consistent Christian life-style, and a church-home program of support and mutual enrichment, we will only have a negative answer to our Lord's question in Luke 18:8: "When the Son of Man comes, will He find faith on the earth?" We are in an age in which churches could well be compared to Israel as described by 2 Kings 17:33 (*New American Standard Bible*)—"They feared the Lord and served their own gods according to the custom of the nations from among whom they had been carried away into exile."

Many of today's evangelical churches have come to realize that a large number of the problems that do arise within the church are caused by poor procedures, ill-defined jobs, confused communication, and other organizational weaknesses. In the past, we have simply said, "It was sin," "Christians shouldn't act that way," or have used some other common phrase to dismiss a problem we believed was unsolvable unless a great spiritual revival would take place.

Although moral corruption is the ultimate cause of all of man's inability to get along with others, many of our organizational problems today are not necessarily the results of direct and immediate personal sin but are the failure to use the tools and skills that God has put at our disposal to allow us to function productively as human beings in organizational relationships. Those tools and skills are a reflection of the very nature and attributes of God. They include such things as clear communication, design, purpose, goals, organization, and rules or controls for proper behavior.

Later in this volume we will deal more specifically with some of the skills and procedures that consultants can and do use to help churches carry out their functions in an orderly and productive manner. There are a few things that should be noted at this juncture, however, to put in perspective the material that follows.

Note that the exercise of management principles and practices is not a substitute for the ministry of the Holy Spirit of God in believers' lives. Rather, it is a set of guidelines and activities designed to produce an orderly and properly functioning group. All motives, methods, and desired outcomes must be under the guidance and approval of God. What is clearly needed is for individuals and groups to be spiritually aligned with the Lord as they carry out their activities in a positive and proper manner.

Another factor that should be recognized is that pastors or churches who seek consultative help in carrying out their ministries are operating from positions of strength. The Scriptures instruct us to seek the counsel and wisdom of other believers. In so doing we should turn to those who have a good reputation and experience in the areas of need. In so doing we build up one another to greater godliness and service.

When it comes to a style of leadership or ministry, there is no single biblical model. There are common spiritual qualifications and godly attitudes that all true

Christian leaders must demonstrate, such as those set forth in 1 Timothy 2; 2 Timothy 2; Titus 1; and Matthew 20. A person's style of leadership, however, is that characteristic behavior that is an expression of a combination of factors—personality, prior experience, formal and informal training, and circumstances. An effective leader should be able to identify and get the most from his characteristics but also be flexible enough to modify his leadership style to fit the needs and expectations of the group. Leadership is never static. It is an ever-changing and adjusting experience.

Objectives are also essential ingredients in a properly functioning church ministry, for they provide both motivation and evaluative criteria. It is unfortunate that in most Christian organizations there are no carefully thought out objectives but only a series of programs that are seldom evaluated as to their true value.

One final major concern is the matter of organizational integration and interdependent support. That can best be studied from a systems management viewpoint. Once an organization understands the multiple forces that affect its actual operation, it can better pinpoint problems and make necessary adjustments. Also, the ability to project the financial needs of a group on the basis of projected programs makes individuals and groups more aware of their actual needs and more fiscally responsible.

The church today is in need. It needs the reviving of inner strength that comes from a total commitment to the inerrant Word of God and to the God of the Word. It needs a refreshing touch from the Holy Spirit, who delights in pointing people to Jesus Christ, our Lord and Savior. It needs the revitalization that comes from a careful and thorough analysis of its purpose (reason for existence), its goals and objectives (those measurable and controllable targets toward which it should move), its programs (those diverse activities that are grounded in history and culture, but necessary to its effective operation), and its results (those Christ-mandated teachings of Scripture).

Churches are organizations and, as such, are subject to change, both development and decay. As with our personal health, it is a good practice to see a physician periodically for a checkup. That is preventative or developmental consultation. The same is needed in churches and other types of organizations.

Obviously, when a person is sick and hurting, a physician is necessary. So also with an organization. A consultant is one who, like a physician, attempts to diagnose institutional illness on the basis of what a church tells him and the instruments he uses. In the following chapter, the concept, role, function, and activity of the consultant are considered.

2

The Consulting Process

"We've always had a good ministry in this location, but recently offerings are declining and our attendance is dropping. Other churches in our community seem to be growing properly. What's wrong with us?" That special plea for help in time of need is not uncommon in many churches today.

"We have grown from one hundred to five fifty in the past three years, and we don't know what to do about leadership training, nor do we know what we should do with regard to building and facilities. Can you give us some help along this line?" A second church needs help, not because of decline, but because of growth.

"Nobody is talking to anybody anymore! On Sunday mornings you can just feel the tensions within the church. The pastor hardly gets along with the board, and the board won't tell the congregation what's going on. Nobody talks to anybody around here anymore!" This church is going through various struggles, and crisis is imminent. It needs help but does not know where to turn for it.

"Pastor Jones was with us for fifteen years, and we had a very solid ministry all during that period of time. He has now told us that the Lord is leading him to another church in another state, and we were wondering if you could help us in finding what type of pastor would best meet our needs and the kind of ministry that we should be having?" A normal change process has affected the fourth church and they, too, are seeking advice.

The common denominator in all four churches is the need for some consultative help. In the first and third churches, the problems are of crisis proportions; in the second and fourth churches, the problems are less crisis-oriented.

Sometimes help is sought by a single individual, such as a pastor or the chairman of the board of the church, in the same way that an individual seeks legal counsel from a lawyer or medical counsel from a physician. In such cases, the helping procedure is highly personalized and individualistic. At other times, the board or congregation seeks consultative help. In that situation, the consultant must deal with the group as a group, seeking information from all involved, and delivering information to all involved.

CONSULTANT DEFINED

A consultant is one who aids individuals, groups, organizations, or even larger combinations of organizations in diagnosing the real problems that exist, gathering the appropriate data and information necessary to deal with the problems, suggesting alternate solutions to particular problems, and ultimately assisting in the mobilization of both internal and external resources to solve the problems.

There are internal consultants within some larger organizations, whose function it is to aid in a particular department or to serve the entire organization as an internal observer-evaluator and helper. Normally, however, consultants are individuals brought in from the outside to aid the organization by giving expert advice, providing objective evaluation, and by providing the assistance and support necessary for handling particular problems.

Efficiency ought to characterize the Bible-believing and Christ-honoring church. Since time is one of our most precious commodities, doing the Lord's work the right way is crucial.

Effectiveness ought also to characterize the ministry of the church, because doing the right things is even more important than doing things the right way.

Every organization, if it is to be vital and viable, needs to be periodically examined and evaluated. Even healthy organizations need to identify their strong and weak points. A consultant's job is primarily to help an organization maximize its strengths and eliminate its weaknesses. It is a helping ministry from start to finish.

BENEFITS OF A CONSULTATION PROGRAM

There are many pluses in hiring a consultant to work with an organization, whether it be a church, a mission, a school, or a business. First and foremost, a consultant is an objective helper who, as an outsider, can see things that others who have worked with the organization are often unable to see. When people have lived with and tolerated something for many, many years, they become so accustomed to it that they do not perceive difficulties or problems. The consultant from the outside can be objective, and as an observer can point out many oversights and areas that overlap. He can properly question many practices that have been accepted as valid, even though the results seem presently not to indicate their validity. The consultant benefits the organization by asking questions that normally would not be asked by insiders.

Another benefit of a consultation program is that the consultant can be an information specialist, providing the organization with research data that it would not ordinarily be acquainted with. Through his preparation and study and through experience, the consultant has available information on organizational development, behavioral science, and sociological research to use in a flexible way with each organization or group that he serves. The consultant usually has access to various instruments for data gathering and the ability to interpret those instruments properly before the organization so that it can get the most value from the data.

A consultant is an asset to an organization as a trainer/ educator. Helping others to do their work the right way is one of the real joys of a consultation ministry. To see inefficient procedures become efficient, and to see ineffective goals become effective, is indeed a very thrilling experience for both the consultant and the organization.

Another value in a consultation program is the role the consultant plays as an enabler in providing the proper atmosphere and development process for effective change. Individuals within an organization need help from the right source to gain a new perspective on an old problem, and the consultant as an enabler can help to accomplish that.

A final benefit of having a consultant for an organization is the role that the consultant can play in problem solving. The consultant can participate with the leadership and the people in discussing various vital issues without an emotional attachment to the problem, and can offer alternative suggestions without fear of being forever linked with that particular idea in that particular setting.

He helps build bridges between problems and solutions and between old ideas and new ones. Being vitally interested but emotionally uninvolved, the consultant can help individuals and groups within an organization see other people's perspectives more effectively than can someone whose role and responsibility within the organization is clearly defined.

LIMITATIONS OF THE CONSULTANT PROGRAM

Although there are many benefits to a consulting program, there are some limitations that should be mentioned. Much is expected of a consultant when a relationship is established with an organization. Some people envision in that person the complete solution to all their ills. Obviously that is not the case. Sometimes the high expectation level established by some individuals causes them to oversimplify the issue or issues that are involved in the problem.

A second limitation in a consultant's role is that a consultant is a helper and is not one who should do the work or make the vital decisions in place of the leadership and people of the organization. Many churches and missions expect a consultant to make the decisions for them and to implement those decisions. That is very difficult for an outsider to accomplish, and where the expectation level is of that type, the consultation process often breaks down.

A third problem is related to the first in that because individuals often expect problems to be handled quickly, they also expect pat or simple answers to complex problems. It must be recognized that most problems that bring crisis in an organization have developed over a long period of time and have many different roots. If each of those is to be properly traced and handled, time and multiple approaches will have to be used. There are no simple, pat answers to most organizational problems.

One final problem that arises in a consultation relationship is the expectation that the consultant is an expert in every area of organizational need. Problems will range from finances to interpersonal relationships, as well as other more mechanical issues. No one person has ultimate knowledge in each area, and often others will need to be brought into the advisory relationship if the problem is to be properly solved. If a consultant does not give quick, prescriptive, simple, and yet complex answers, there is often an air of disappointment. That presents the consultant and the total process with a major hurdle that is very difficult to overcome. An organization needs to have a realistic attitude toward the total problem-solving and helping process.

APPROACHES TO CONSULTATION

There are many different roles that a consultant takes as he is engaged to work through a problem with a client. The consultant is really intervening in a situation that may be of low intensity, not involving crisis, or one with a high intensity problem that involves a major crisis. The point at which the consultant enters into the relationship affects greatly the role the consultant takes with the client.

ILLUSTRATION FOR APPROACHES

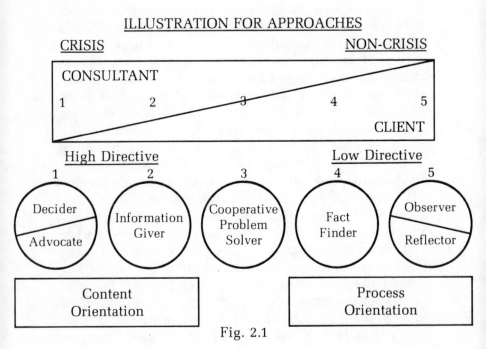

Fig. 2.1

Figure 2.1 presents a continuum showing five different roles a consultant can take depending upon the intensity of the situation. On the left there is a high profile involvement of the consultant, whose first activity is that of a decider/advocate. When a church or organization is in a crisis, there is need for someone to act as a stabilizer, propose guidelines, persuade, and even give direct advice as to what should be done. The role is very directive and is highly content oriented.

When the consultant enters into a situation that is not in crisis, the consultant usually takes an observer/ reflector role. He is not directive, but helps the church or organization to identify the problems, points them in the direction of where data in the problem-solving process can be found, and helps them to work through the process of problem solving. Here the emphasis is on process, with the consultant taking more of an educator/counselor role.

Between the two potential extremes of crisis and non-crisis, or high directive and low directive leadership on the part of the consultant, are three other possibilities. Where there is a midpoint in the level of consultant activity, the consultant is in a moderate crisis situation, assisting the organization by cooperative problem solving. The consultant helps the organization and leaders define goals, perceive the situation as accurately as possible, suggest alternative routes to solutions, provide links to other existing resources, and helps to divide the problem into smaller and more manageable units.

The more the problem tends toward crisis, the more the consultant tends to be an information giver (the number 2 position on the chart), providing the organization with data in a brief and concise form to which they would not readily have access. The consultant tends also to give information regarding policies or procedures that should be followed to effectively bring the situation under control. The difference between the information giver and the decider/advocate is simply in the level of activity that the consultant takes.

The number 4 position identified on the chart as fact finder is the role a consultant takes when he assists the organization by interviewing its key people, reviewing the documents and records of the organization, and providing informational instruments, such as check lists and questionnaires. He observes the operation and analyzes and summarizes the data so that it can be properly digested by the client. The role here is one of giving information and allowing the client to be the deciding person or group, thus making the client responsible for his actions.

In any consultation experience, although one may enter into the problem at any one of the points on the continuum, a professionally trained consultant will move up and down the continuum since no consultation remains long at any one point. Every consultation will involve addressing many different problems, and each one may be at a different point on the crisis continuum level. A consultant may be dealing with an organization that has many different problems, and will therefore be using many different approaches. To be aware of the various alternatives, and to be wise in the use of the skills related to each one, is extremely important to any properly functioning consultant.

The Qualifications of a Consultant

As can be seen from what is involved in the consulting process and the types of behavior and skills necessary for a proper consultation, it is fitting that we consider some of the characteristics and qualifications that are necessary if a person is to be an effective consultant.

It goes without saying that a consultant should be knowledgeable of the literature, philosophy, principles, and practices of a consultation ministry. Today there is a continuing flood of information in the realm of proper institutional and independent consultation. Having an understanding of psychology, sociology, and organizational and business practices is vital. For the one who is to consult with churches and missions, a good knowledge of theology, church polity, and nonprofit organizational functioning is essential.

The motive behind any consultation must be service to

the client. If the consultant's primary concern is financial gain, that preoccupation can take away from the effectiveness of the consultation.

The American Society for Training and Development has published a code of ethics for consultants. It includes such items as: not violating the confidences of the client, limiting activities to areas of the client's expertise, making sure that facts are properly presented and accurate in detail, and conducting oneself and one's activities in such a way that there will be no embarrassment or disparagement to the client in the process.

In addition to those general points, it should be obvious that the consultant should be one whose knowledge and expertise has been gained through both careful formal study and successful practical experience. Many individuals want to share knowledge and help others when they themselves have not successfully performed in their church or work. A client should carefully check out the track record of the consultant to insure that the experience and knowledge gained will be helpful to him in the problem-solving process. A client should also check to be sure that the personality of the consultant is one that will mesh and blend properly with the needs of the organization and leaders that will be involved in the process of consultation.

The consultant must always act with integrity, adhere to professional standards required of consultants, and respect the right and reputation of the organization with which he is associated. To consult with an organization is indeed a privilege, and to see that organization progress and develop as a result of your involvement with them is indeed a thrilling experience.

PROCEDURES IN ESTABLISHING A CONSULTATION

It is wise in establishing a consultation, whether on the part of the consultant or on the part of the organization, to be sure that there is clear communication and understanding with regard to what is involved in the consulting process. For that reason, specifying a series of steps with specified targets and a time limit is extremely helpful. Seven steps are suggested here as the workable framework for a typical consultation relationship.

1. INITIATING THE PROCESS

Consultations are initiated in several different ways. At times a consultant, in seeking clients and working relationships, will introduce himself via advertising, brochures, personal contacts, or by telephone to different organizations or individuals that he feels would benefit significantly from his expertise. A second way in which contacts are made are when organizations seeking specified help contact consultants concerning their needs and proposals for a working relationship. A third way consultations are arranged is through a third party. Someone who sees the need in a particular organization and knows of the skills of a particular consultant will get the two parties together.

Regardless of how the consulting relationship is initiated, it is very important that in the early contact the consultant evaluate the situation and determine whether or not he has the resources and skills to properly advise and assist the organization. That will involve some conversation, exploration of basic data regarding the organization, and an analysis of the time that will be involved in carrying out the necessary working arrangement.

It becomes clear that in this early step, because of the skills and abilities that are needed, a consultant must be one who can see quickly the needs of a particular organization. It may appear obvious that the consultant should have insight and perception; the ability to simplify the complex; the ability to separate major from minor issues; and the ability to effectively communicate, motivate, coordinate, supervise, and ultimately manage his time and the people in the organization to accomplish positive end results; but those are critical abilities that are essential and need to be specifically considered. If the problem in the organization is of crisis proportions, the consultant must also have the ability to see solutions to "insoluble" problems.

At the early stage in a relationship, a degree of confidence must be established between the organization and the consultant so that step 2 can be realized.

2. FORMULATING THE AGREEMENT

Consultants work in different ways, but it is always wise to have in writing what is agreed to between the consultant and the organization. At times that can take the form of a formal contract with specified services delineated, costs and expenses projected, and a time frame established, and the entire agreement properly authorized by the appropriate parties.

At other times, the agreement can be a series of paragraphs that spells out the guidelines under which the consultant will be working with the organization and the financial arrangements (if any) that are involved in such situations. Because the consultant is going to be investing time, wisdom, and effort in the pursuit of solutions to the problems within the organization, proper remuneration should be considered.

The agreement should be not only signed by the consultant but agreed to by the governing body of the organization and countersigned by the appropriate individual in the organization who is authorized to complete such legal arrangements.

3. IDENTIFYING THE PROBLEM(S)

Once the consulting process is begun, one of the first primary responsibilities of the consultant is to identify and separate major problems from minor ones. That involves a careful diagnosis of the situation and the separation of issues into organizational, communication, financial, and other categories. Each issue must then be evaluated in terms of time invested, priority of attention, and the allocation of resources to appropriately handle the problem. This is a preliminary step in the ultimate planning process of the total working plan for problem solving. It is also probably the most important step in the process, because much time and energy is inefficiently used trying to find solutions to problems that do not exist. The consultant must be seeking answers to viable questions.

4. GATHERING THE DATA

The consultant must be a data gatherer and analyzer. Through the use of questionnaires, checklists, interviewing, and studying of past reports, minutes, and other data, the consultant will glean information necessary to assist in solving the primary problems of the organization. That data also needs to be sorted as to validity and priority.

The consultant is interested both in facts and opinions, and must be one who can distinguish between the two. Both are valuable, since opinions of individuals within organizations have a significant effect upon the morale, atmosphere, and direction of the organization.

5. ESTABLISHING THE GOALS AND PLAN OF ACTION

Once the data has been gathered and sorted, the primary targets should be identified and a plan of action developed to guide the continuing consulting relationship. It should be noted that steps 1 through 5 in a crisis situation are often extremely intensive steps and must be taken in a short amount of time. Once the immediate crisis situation has been handled, then steps 3, 4, and 5 should be redone to obtain a broader picture of the actual needs of the organization.

Specific goals should be set in each of the problem areas that have been identified in step 3. Those may also be set in terms of major and minor goals. For each goal there needs to be a plan that identifies what action is to be taken, who is to take the action, and the expected results. A plan that will work must also have in it a cost analysis in terms of the time of individuals, monies, facilities, equipment, and materials.

6. IMPLEMENTING THE PLAN

"Plan the work and then work the plan," someone has wisely said. If time permits, it is wise to develop a P.E.R.T.* chart to indicate the process that is being employed in the identification and carrying out of the plan. Action should be taken by those who have the right and authority to do so. Information must be fed back throughout the entire organization so that everyone is kept aware of what progress is being made in the consultative arrangement. An exception would be when the consultation is with a single individual, such as a chief executive officer of the organization, in which the relationship is a private and professional one, akin to a lawyer or physician consulting with a client. In cases, however, where the consultant deals with a church, mission, school, or other such organization where there are many individuals involved, all must be kept notified of progress if morale and health is to be maintained.

7. EVALUATING THE ACTION

The consultant process involving the steps taken in the organization needs to be reviewed in order to formulate further action. At times the initial action will be sufficient to solve the problem and release the consultant from responsibilities. In that case there should be a clear-cut break between the consultant and the organization, and the organization should carry on its own continuing evaluation.

*Program Evaluation Review Technique. See Louis A. Allen, *The Management Profession* (New York: McGraw-Hill, 1964), pp. 139-45.

At times major objectives will have been achieved, but minor ones will have not, and the organization will desire to have the consultant continue in a working relationship over a specified period of time. That should be spelled out in a new agreement.

Consultation is a helping relationship. Seeing an organization turned around and moving from a negative to a positive posture is indeed an exciting experience. If the consultation is with an individual, then the rewards are more personalized as individuals grow and reach the potential for which God has intended them. Seeking counsel is indeed biblical. Giving counsel demands the best from each consultant. Every precaution should be taken to insure that this helping relationship is clear, ethical in every detail, and carried out to the best of one's ability.

3

Faith Chapel: Crisis in a Small Independent Church

This case study covers an actual consultation experience in a small independent church. The church had personal, sociological, financial, spiritual, and management problems that brought it to the brink of chaos. When reading the case study, note the different types of problems and steps taken in this situation.

THE HISTORICAL AND GEOGRAPHICAL ORIENTATION OF THE CHURCH

Faith Chapel was started as a branch of a large independent church. It is located in a suburb of a large city. Most of its members live in the general location of the church.

The first pastor was called to the church in 1945. He had been serving as a member of the staff at a nearby church. At the request of the families starting the new work, and with the blessing of the pastor, he assumed leadership of the new group. The group met for a time without a formal organization and then later became incorporated as an independent church. The pastor had a somewhat limited educational background. He was sincere, theologically conservative, and unmarried.

When the group did establish a formal organization, the pastor was designated to be the one in control. A church board of ten members, which became self-perpetuating, was established by the pastor. The pastor and the church board formed a church constitution that stipulated that the board members alone were church members. They were the only ones who could hold office and vote. All committees of the church must be made up of board members. An official fellowship was formed of those others who attended and supported the church. The extent of their official standing included the fact that their names would be on the fellowship list. They had no voice or vote.

One of the board members served as church treasurer. When he was out of town, the pastor would care for the finances. Only the board received financial reports.

In 1955, the minutes show that the board became rather dissatisfied with the pastoral ministry of their leader. They made some very specific suggestions for changes, which evidenced their dissatisfaction. There were several "constructive criticisms." The board noted in writing that those must be followed until the board should agree otherwise.

The deficiencies in the ministry were corrected for a time. Later the former methods of ministry were reinstated by the pastor. The board did not officially raise its voice, although there was a strong undercurrent of disagreement.

By 1962, the group was considering the construction of a new sanctuary. At that time the church's name was changed. The earlier dissatisfaction with the pastor's ministry had evidently diminished, for the board at that point not only voted to build a new sanctuary but also agreed to start a retirement plan for the pastor and to make provision for his hospitalization beyond his salary.

The new sanctuary was constructed largely under the guidance of a contractor who had joined the fellowship of the church. He had been seriously ill in the hospital, and the pastor had visited him regularly and prayed with him. The contractor made a covenant with God in which he

pledged to build a new church for that group of worshipers if he were allowed to recover from his illness. He did
recover, and spent much time and money to fulfill his
promise. He was a member of the church fellowship, but
not a member of the board. Through the period of illness
and recovery and the construction of the sanctuary, he
became very close to the pastor. The close relationship
between the two men affected many of the later activities
in the church.

PRECIPITATING FACTORS OF THE CHURCH CRISIS

Several men with professional leadership capability
were added to the membership of the board. Those men
held leadership positions in the secular organizations in
which they were employed. In management terms, that
would be referred to as a "latent culture"—one in which
the background was quite different educationally, professionally, and culturally from that of most of the people
who had been attending the church since its inception.
Their families had been attending the church partly due
to its proximity to their homes but more especially because of its conservative theological position.

Once they assumed positions on the board, the men
realized that the organizational structure of the church
was very narrow and authoritarian. They began to question the way things were being done and sought to make
some changes. They also began to question the wisdom of
some of the decisions being made by the pastor. They
believed very definitely that the pastor was not providing
a pulpit ministry that would edify the congregation.

The board tried on numerous occasions to discuss their
feelings with the pastor but without satisfactory results.
On more than one occasion, he had resigned rather than
face the possibility of having to make changes in the
church organizational structure and in his method of
ministry. Each time the board backed down and refused to
accept his resignation. It was very evident by now that the

changes were not going to be implemented. The pastor resigned again, and at that point the board accepted the resignation.

A few members on the church board and several members of the church fellowship were very upset because of the board's acceptance of the resignation. One of them was the contractor who had been instrumental in building the new sanctuary and who was a personal friend of the pastor.

The church gave the pastor a substantial severance gift that provided, among other things, a large part of the finances for an extensive tour.

The board now had the responsibility of directing the church. Of the board members who had voted against the acceptance of the pastor's resignation, all but one resigned. Tensions began to mount, and two distinct groups were formed. One group had favored the acceptance of the pastor's resignation, and the other group had opposed it. It is said that at one point, board members were locked by the dissenting group within a room. On another occasion the church was picketed. During a Sunday morning service, one of the attendants stood to his feet in the service and asked why the leader of the service had not remembered the former pastor in the morning prayer. The individual refused to be seated until the leaders threatened to forcibly eject him from the service.

During the turmoil, the former pastor was traveling. The group that had left the fellowship of the church saw that there was a good possibility that the former pastor would not be asked to return to the pastorate. The contractor wired to the former pastor and asked that he return to the city immediately, hoping that the pastor's presence would alter the situation. His request showed the sharp feelings still in existence. Telephones rang throughout the community, and rumors gathered momentum. It became very difficult to separate fact from fiction. Vehement accusations were made against the members of the board who had voted to accept the pastor's resignation.

THE POINT OF CONTACT BETWEEN THE CHURCH
AND THE CONSULTANT

When the pastor finally resigned and officially left the pastorate of the church, the board engaged pulpit supplies. That meant there was a different preacher each Sunday, with no one to take the midweek service and no one to be in charge during the week. The board realized the need for having an interim pastor in order to stabilize the church situation.

The name of a consultant was given to the chairman of the board by a friend. The board chairman called, and the consultant accepted the invitation to preach for two Sundays. After the first Sunday evening service, the consultant and his wife were invited to the home of the church chairman for an informal time of fellowship. Though unknown to the consultant, the members of the pulpit committee had also been invited. They told the consultant of the rather critical condition of their church and asked if the consultant would be willing to serve as an interim pastor and church consultant for a time. He notified them the next Sunday that he would be willing to do what he could. That marked the beginning of some very strenuous weeks.

As interim pastor, the consultant had no responsibility for the visitation program of the church, conducting funerals, or performing weddings. He did have the administrative responsibilities a pastor would normally have. It was also his responsibility to preach each Sunday morning and evening. Attendance at board meetings was mandatory, and attendance at committee meetings was optional. That arrangement was approved by the board.

PROBLEMS EXPOSED AND PROCEDURES FOLLOWED
DURING THE CONSULTATION

LEADERSHIP DEFICIENCIES

One of the primary problems at Faith Chapel was the lack of trained leadership. It became evident at once that there was good leadership potential, but the former pastor had not given individuals opportunity to develop that potential. Motives should not be imputed, but the evidence seemed to indicate that the pastor may have felt threatened. Many of his laymen had far more education than he. They had also attained postions of leadership in their companies. It was quite evident that they could assume far more responsibility and leadership in the church if given a chance. Not only was the pastor threatened as a person, but his power over the organization was also at stake. The organizational structure of the church, which had been created by the pastor, gave evidence of his desire for control. It may seem to be an unusual arrangement, but many churches are organized so that the pastor has complete control.

The pastor's was the only type of leadership seen by those who attended the church. When he left, a leadership crisis arose. The laymen had not been trained in church administration. Since they had not had opportunities to lead, the church attendants did not regard or respect their leadership. Those who were now forced by circumstances to assume leadership had to be trained, and the congregation had to develop a respect for their leadership.

Due to the leadership crisis, it was necessary for the church consultant to assume the reins of leadership. It is not normally wise for a consultant to make decisions, but in crisis consultation that is often necessary until leaders can be trained. Democracy is a slow process, and in crisis consultation the time is limited.

The leadership role assumed by the consultant was quite different from the one assumed by the former pastor. The consultant worked very closely with the board to train them so that later they could make decisions on their own. They began to report all decisions to the church attendants through the church bulletin.

The consultant made clear to the board and to the

members of the congregation that he had confidence in
the ability and judgment of the board. That encouraged
the board members and brought a feeling of stability to
the congregation.

Before each board meeting, the consultant spent time
with the chairman of the board. They discussed procedures to be followed at the meeting, and analyzed the
matters to come before the board. The chairman had had
experience in leading company business meetings but
found that was quite different from leading board meetings of a volunteer organization.

Books and mimeographed materials were provided by
the consultant for all members of the board. The men
were encouraged to read the material on their own. The
materials were not discussed in the board meeting. Board
members could gain knowledge of church administration
on their own without giving public evidence of their ig-
norance at various points. It was important to let them
"save face." Their reading would also acquaint them with
the reasoning behind certain steps that were being taken
by the consultant.

Two members of the board assisted in the worship services each Sunday. That conveyed to the members of the
congregation in an indirect way that the board members
were assuming leadership roles. It developed their confidence and competence. The board members became more
sympathetic toward the work of the pastor as they assumed a portion of his activity. One of the board members
who helped with the worship services had been the
pastor of another church for some years. He had left
pastoral work and gone into secular work for financial
reasons. He was still interested in pastoral work, however,
so helping in worship services gave him an opportunity
to have a part. He has since returned to a pastorate and
left the secular employment.

Members of the board were stationed at the church en-
trances before and after the services to greet the people.

That gave the attendants an opportunity to have personal contact with the board members and to get to know them better.

Some of the board members took charge of the midweek service. Their lack of development in that area was soon evident. A change was then made so that the consultant took the Bible study portion of the midweek service, which was preceded by a prayer time led by the board members.

NEED FOR LAY INVOLVEMENT

There were several organizational problems that hampered the process of revitalization.* One of the major ones centered in the church constitution, which indicated that all church business was to be controlled by the board. That board was self-perpetuating and was under the domination of the pastor. Since the board members were the only church members, each time the board had a meeting, that was considered a *church* meeting. Only church members could be on the church committees. Therefore all committees were composed of board members.

It became evident at once that some changes had to be made in the constitution so that the people might have a voice in the governing of the church. The strict board control became a helpful factor in the time of constitutional reconstruction. The proposed changes had only to pass the board to become "law."

The consultant did not seek to change the constitution immediately. He proposed that the board merely bypass those parts of the constitution that restricted leadership to the board and proceed to develop a working arrangement involving the members of the congregation. Because there were only a couple of copies of the constitu-

*For more information on church revitalization, see Lloyd M. Perry, *Getting the Church on Target* (Chicago: Moody, 1977), pp. 7-8.

tion available, those attending the church were really not aware of its contents. During that time of bypassing the constitution, the board would survey other constitutions and formulate a new constitution for Faith Chapel. They could then make the adjustments they saw were needed. The suggestion passed with no negative vote, and they proceeded accordingly.

It was difficult to believe that the people had been willing to attend the church for all those years without having a voice in its government. It was only possible because most of them had not known any other type of church. They had not realized how other churches were controlled. Although the former pastor had formulated a fellowship list of church attendants, those on the list had not realized that actually they had nothing to say about the operation of the church. The pastor had been there for many years. He had performed their marriages and conducted funerals for members of their families. They had, for many years, accepted his rule without question. Questions began to arise later as new people came to the church from other groups, which happens naturally with the influx of a latent (different socially and economically) culture.

COMMUNICATION COMPLICATIONS

Communication complications played a large role in establishing a foundation for the church crisis. The congregation did not have copies of the constitution. That meant they did not have an opportunity to see the organizational restrictions. They did not receive financial reports, because such matters were cared for by the "membership"—only the ten board members received the reports. The church had not used church bulletins for its services, so there was no channel for conveying information to the people.

It became evident at once that the board and the church attendants had to have some communication so that everyone could be familiar with the general situation. The consultant, with the board, instituted the policy that there would no longer be any administrative secrets. Several steps were taken to make that slogan a reality.

The church started using church bulletins for the Sunday services. The board asked the consultant to select the material to be used. The bulletin provided space in which they could refute error. Whenever they heard of rumors being circulated by people formerly connected with the church, they would put the facts in the bulletin, thus keeping the truth before the people. Names were not used, merely facts, and people soon realized that it was not profitable to circulate rumors that were not factual.

The church board organized a fellowship time after an evening service and provided refreshments. The church attendants were the guests of the board members. The announced purpose of the meeting was to hear a report from the church consultant regarding the general church situation. The consultant went over matters with the board prior to the meeting so that there would be no surprises for the board members.

The board distributed copies of the old constitution to all of the church attendants present. It was pointed out that within the constitution only the board members were *members* of the church and that the others were listed in the church *fellowship* but had no voting power. Those in attendance agreed immediately that something must be done to rectify a rather desperate situation. That evening they informally gave a vote of confidence to the board.

There was a lack of communication not only between the church board and the attendants but also between various age groups within the church. One of the older couples who had worked in the church for many years decided that they should leave and join the group of former fellowship members who were attending a neighboring church. It came to light that at least one elderly lady believed that the younger ladies did not care for the elderly. Although the consultant had not observed that to be the case, the complaint was noted.

The younger women in the church presented to the church board a proposal that had been discussed with the church consultant. The younger ladies were to invite the older ladies of the church to spend a day with them at a nearby village. The younger ladies would provide the transportation, and each would take one of the older ladies as her special guest. The day included a shopping tour, sight-seeing, and a special luncheon at a unique restaurant. The bill, including the transportation and luncheon for the entire group, was to be paid by the church. The actual cost was not really great—the friendship and understanding established were beyond financial value. Possibly no single venture during those transitory months at the church created more understanding between people than did the excursion.

There had been few lines of communication established between the church and the community. The church had a strong youth program that provided physical, social, and spiritual training for the young people of the church and community. Few contacts were being made in the homes of those young people. In former years, the church had sponsored suppers for the young people and their parents. The parents had been asked to contribute to the suppers by giving food and money.

The church changed its approach and invited the youth and their parents to be the guests of the church for a supper and for a magic program held following the supper. The men and women of the church served the supper and provided the food. The supper and program were well attended. When the parents of the young people asked if they could help finance the supper and program, the church people explained that they wanted to do it themselves out of appreciation for having the opportunity to become better acquainted. That established with the community a link of friendship that has developed and grown.

The communication had been so poor between the administration and the church attendants that the church office and pastor's study had been off limits except to the board members. The consultant and board worked for some time to get those two locations cleaned, painted, and refurbished. New office equipment was purchased, and new cabinets were installed. When the renovations were completed, the board held an open house so that all on the church fellowship list could see the entire facility. Seeing the improvements enhanced the feeling of ownership on the part of the church constituency.

It was important to establish two-way communication between the church administration and the church attendants. The board arranged for several fellowship hours to be held after the evening services. The church people were given opportunity to express to the board areas of church life that they felt needed improvement. They were also given opportunity to make positive suggestions that the board might implement to improve the effectiveness of the church. That type of exchange and sharing increased the spirit of friendliness within the fellowship.

ADMINISTRATIVE PROBLEMS

Among the administrative problems was the lack of job descriptions. The consultant started to correct that deficiency by establishing a job description for the new church secretary. A possible job description was brought to the board, and they were to change it in any way they saw fit. They made only one or two minor changes in it. A copy of the job description is included in Appendix 1. They then suggested that it would be a good idea to have job descriptions for all of the church workers. Each church worker was asked to put in writing the actual activities in which he was engaged. Those were given to the board chairman and the church consultant. They were then arranged and published. They have been changed as conditions have warranted.

It became necessary to bypass the constitution for the time being in the area of committee membership and responsibilities. Membership on the committees was expanded to include interested attendants rather than just board members. The committee structure had not really been operative. There were now many tasks for the committees to carry out as lay people began to assume responsibility with authority. They started with some basic responsibilities for each committee, to which they kept adding as the need arose. Committee responsibilities developed out of experience rather than from assignment by the administration.

The problem in the area of finances was not that of raising money but in reporting and regulating its expenditure. The church owed only a small amount on its building and had over $30,000 in the bank. No one except the former pastor and a few of the board members knew of the balance. The church had not had a budget. The people kept giving but did not know how it was being used. Each organization within the church had its own treasurer and took care of its own finances.

During the time of unrest within the church, the giving had fallen off. The people were beginning to question where their money was going. The consultant discussed with the board the possibility of having a unified budget for the church. Each organization within the church prepared an estimate of its needs for the coming year. The concept of the unified budget was explained to them. Each group would turn in all offerings to the church treasurer, and he would assume the payment of all its bills, up to the extent of its budget. If more money was needed, the organization could appeal to the finance committee.

The board took the concept to the church attendants at a fellowship hour and asked for their reaction, although they still had no vote. It was a move toward establishing a working relationship between the board and congregation, which was to emanate from the new constitution when adopted. The congregation believed that a unified budget would be a good idea, and the board at its next meeting voted to institute it. It was then mimeographed for the entire church to see and follow as a guide.

A minor financial problem had developed due to the fact that the board had never established a cash flowchart. There were a few building bonds to be redeemed, and, in the absence of a cash flowchart, the demand for money was coming at inconvenient times. A cash flowchart was established, and the bond payments were arranged so that there would be money enough in the current fund to cover them as well as meet the current bills.

Through the years, money had been given to the church for memorial gifts. No record had been kept of the specific memorials or monies. The money had been added to the general church funds. As the problems within the church began to come to light, it was evident that that procedure had disturbed a number of people. The board proceeded to seek to discover the extent of those memorial gifts. After several months of research, a list was established. The board then voted to purchase a mahogany plaque with bronze plates to be engraved with the names of the donors of the memorial gifts. The plaque was dedicated at a public service and is now displayed in the church.

Problems arose regarding the counting of the offerings. During the former pastorate, the pastor and a board member had served as treasurers and had counted the offerings. The board now had a regular treasurer and a finance committee. Some of the members of the finance committee lived at a distance from the church and found it difficult to find time to make a special trip to the church during the week to count the money. There were some problems with depositing the money in the bank night deposit slot and having the bank count the receipts. Members of the board had counted the offering during the church services in the past, but now they preferred to be in the services. The board solved the problem by purchasing a small, secondhand safe and installing it within a secret location inside the church building. The offerings were then placed in the safe and could be counted at the convenience of the counters.

It had been the custom to allow outside organizations such as mission agencies to come to the church and make presentations of their work. At the close of each presentation an offering would be received. That money was not counted in the church books, however, as a part of the missionary budget commitment to that organization, so the organization would receive its regular allotment from the church in addition to the offering. Several problems resulted. The organization with the most persuasive presentation would get a large offering, which did not necessarily reflect the worth of the project as much as it reflected the power of the presentation. The church was still faced with meeting its budget commitments to all of the missionary organizations on its list. The special offerings tended to take away from the regular missions offerings. The board instituted a ruling that restricted the taking of special offerings without prior consent by the finance committee of the church.

SPIRITUAL NEEDS

There were several surface problems reflecting deeper spiritual needs within the church. Primarily, there was a need for participation in the worship service. The worship committee incorporated a unison call to worship, which involved the participation of the people with the worship leader. That call to worship was printed in the order of service.

At the place to designate the offering, a verse of Scripture that was related to giving was printed in the order of service. The congregation or the pastor would read the verse aloud. That not only increased congregational participation but also showed the worshipers the scriptural basis for giving. The verse was changed each Sunday.

By selecting the hymns carefully, and by labeling them in the order of service, the consultant helped worshipers become acquainted with different types of hymns and their purposes. Three hymns were normally used in the morning worship service. The first was a hymn of exaltation, which emphasized the attributes of God. The second hymn was one of meditation, designed to prepare the worshiper to receive the message. It was often a gospel song with the emphasis upon the one worshiping. The final hymn was listed in the order of service as either a hymn of invitation or of dedication depending upon the primary emphasis of the service.

The order of the evening praise service was not printed in the church bulletin. The consultant and the board felt that publicizing it in the morning would take away much of the anticipation. There was a printed order of service, however, which was mimeographed so that each participant might have a copy. A "master copy" was printed with a number of options open for special music or other variables. Blanks were included so that the one in charge merely had to complete those blanks. They were thus able to mimeograph one basic format that could be used for several weeks. Since each participant had a copy, the service could proceed without introductions.

The church decided not to use the term *announcements*, but instead referred to them as "King's Business." They avoided announcements that could not really be classified as part of the church program. They also established a rule of not repeating announcements orally that were already printed in the bulletin. The laymen gave the items of King's Business. They were less likely to have an extended extemporaneous message about each one than was the preacher.

It was quite amazing to see the dearth of scriptural knowledge on the part of the members of the congregation. The previous ministry had been stronger on exhorta-

tion than on instruction. That need for scriptural instruction was one of several reasons that prompted the church
consultant to become involved in the preaching ministry
of the church during the consultation period. The pulpit
is a channel through which the consultant can provide
much guidance and instructional help. If he does not do
the preaching during the consultation period, there is
always the risk that the pulpit ministry may either
weaken or contradict that which he is trying to accomplish in consultation. That is especially true in crisis
consultation work since the time is so limited.

The consultant also found that it was expedient for him
to lead a Bible study in connection with the midweek
service. The laymen led the time of prayer and praise, and
the consultant led the Bible study. An extensive amount
of mimeographed material was distributed so that those
attending could assemble a notebook of Bible study material. The notebook provided a source of continuing help
for the people. It also provided contextual information for
a background of the preaching ministry. That contact at
the midweek service provided an informal opportunity
for the consultant to meet and converse with the congregation. The people felt that they knew the consultant personally, and they were more willing than they would have
otherwise been to follow his suggestions and provide
support.

UNIQUE PROBLEMS

Each church has some unique problems. A very disturbing incident took place during the first few weeks of
the consultant's contact with the church. The disenchanted group, who had left with the former pastor at the
time of his termination of service, was busy circulating
rumors through the community. They reported some dev-
astating things that supposedly were going on at the
church now that they were no longer there to keep it on
the "straight and narrow" path. Among those rumors was

one to the effect that the "new group" who had "put the pastor out" was really just interested in getting their hands on the property and building. The disenchanted group was interested in finding any possible thread of evidence that might substantiate their rumor.

One evening, the church consultant received a frantic call from one of the staunch supporters of the former pastor. The caller said he had just received a handbill that was one of many being circulated throughout the community. The handbill was advertising a meeting that the local public schools' Parent-Teacher Association was to hold at the church. The next evening they were to hold a fund-raising dance in the church gymnasium, and all in the community were invited to attend. One cannot appreciate the size of this problem unless one realizes that a dance in an ultraconservative church is totally unheard of. The fact that the dance was to be held at the church was in large print, and the fact that it was sponsored by the PTA was in small print.

To the individual who reported it, that activity proved the point that he and his cohorts had been making: the "new" group was really not interested in a spiritual ministry for the church.

How had the incident developed? The church had allowed the PTA to hold some of its business meetings at the church on previous occasions. When the request came for that particular meeting, the board did not dream that it was to be a dance rather than a business meeting. The board member who had granted permission for the meeting on behalf of the church had not asked the right questions.

The consultant arranged for two members of the church board to contact the school principal that evening and explain the dilemma. The principal saw the problem immediately and was very understanding. It was too late, however, to send notices with the students regarding a transfer of location. The principal did call the leaders of the organization and provided space in the school for the party. He also announced the change of location at the opening of school. The church consultant arranged to be at the church the next evening in case any community members came, not having been notified of the change of location.

There was no question in the mind of the consultant that the dance should not be held at the church. He was also convinced that by being present at the church he would provide an encouragement to those who were trying to maintain a spiritual ministry at the church, and would be a deterrent to further trouble that might be caused by the dissenters. It is important that a consultant sense such problems and be willing to share personally in their solutions.

The consultant suspected that there might be some legal problems in connection with the church. As he became aware of the unique type of organizational framework that had developed through the years, he suggested that the board engage a lawyer to look into possible problem areas.

An attorney was contacted. He checked the constitution and bylaws of the church and made a couple of suggestions that should be included here. He discovered that the church did not have clearance from the Internal Revenue Service, which would allow the members to contribute to the church and deduct such gifts from their income tax. That matter was rectified by the lawyer. He also obtained a tax identification number for the church. He obtained for the church a letter from the Department of Revenue establishing the exemption of the church from state and local retailers' occupation tax, and from state and local service occupation tax. The lawyer obtained an affidavit of status of exempt property from the Tax Assessor of that county and made certain that it was properly filed.

There are always psychological problems that appear as a result of a cataclysmic experience such as that which transpired in this church. There was a need for the restoration of confidence in one another. The consultant assisted by giving verbal and behavioral confirmation of his confidence in the leadership and the congregation.

There was a need for hope. The people needed to see positive things happening. They had spent a large amount of money for carpeting for the Sunday school facilities. That had never been put down but had been just piled in the corner. The consultant encouraged the board to get the carpet laid so that the people could see it as one positive step that was being taken. It was in place in a couple of weeks.

Windows that had been broken out in the back of the church were repaired. The church had planned to get a new Communion table but had forgotten about it in the midst of the upset. The consultant encouraged the board to carry through on the project. The pulpit ministry emphasized encouragement. Fellowship times and social gatherings were encouraged at the church so that the people could get to know one another and develop a sense of oneness.

Many of the steps taken by the consultant may at first appear to have been unrelated to the solution of the crisis that faced the church. It should be remembered, however, that a church is a system. A systemic analysis must therefore be undertaken to understand the relationship of the many components that compose that system. Human, physical, monetary, and spiritual resources are blended into organizational structures, which are designed to accomplish a church's ministry goals. Since there is a dynamic relationship between the parts of a system, one can influence the entire system by dealing with its individual parts. No part of a system is isolated from the others.

The Climax of the Consultation Experience

This consultation experience started in March and

came to a climax nine months later. A report by the consultant was mimeographed and given to the people. An outline form was used to avoid verbosity and to highlight the various points. Four main purposes behind the consultation were emphasized, and the objectives were listed under each purpose.

For nine months, the church board had been working toward the day when the church would be organized into a cohesive, active, purposeful body. The church board had been operating officially under the old church constitution.

The board, under the advice of the consultant, prepared a two-page working paper for the congregation. It set forth the two articles of the old constitution (which was still the official one) that gave the power of action to members of the church board. The five resolutions that were presented for adoption were put into writing.

The congregation and board met for the presentation of the paper and for action on the five resolutions in September of 1975. The new pastor had just been called to the church. The church board had cleared all of the procedures and resolutions with him prior to his acceptance of the call. The nature of the resolutions and the content behind each had been discussed with the prospective church membership prior to the meeting. All those affected were made aware of and agreed to the changes before they were instituted.

The first three resolutions, which dealt with the missionary budget, church officers and committees, and the church budget, were to become effective as of January 1, 1976. That gave the new church members time to become acquainted and accustomed to working together before they were faced with extremely important decisions.

The church board had set up the requirements for church membership in accordance with the powers vested in them by the old constitution. They placed the requirements in the *new* constitution to be adopted on September 17. That meant that the sixty new members who had been on the fellowship list and were being received on September 17 met the same membership requirements as those being received at a later date.

The church consultant, in accordance with the vote of the church board, received the sixty members, including the new pastor and his wife, into the church. The new constitution had been officially accepted by the church board, had been discussed with and unofficially accepted by the congregation, and was made effective as of September 17, 1975.

4

Redeemer Community: Crisis in a Medium-Sized Independent Church

THE HISTORICAL AND GEOGRAPHICAL ORIENTATION OF THE CHURCH

When Redeemer Community Church was established in the early 1900s, American Protestantism was in a critical stage in which a conflict between theological liberalism (modernism) and conservatism (fundamentalism) was raging in the major denominations. That debate was a primary force in making Redeemer Community what it is today. B. K. Kuiper, in *The Church in History* ([Grand Rapids: Eerdmans, 1951] p. 469), gives helpful insight into that period:

> In the year 1910, a series of twelve small volumes was published under the title *The Fundamentals: A Testimony to the Truth*. The appearance of these books marked the beginning of the Fundamentalist Movement, an organized attempt to uphold the teachings of the Bible against Modernism. The doctrines set forth in these books as fundamental were: (1) the Bible's freedom from error in every respect, (2) the virgin birth of Christ, (3) the substitutionary work of Christ on the cross (that He suffered and died in our stead to satisfy the wrath of God against sin), (4) the physical resurrection, and (5) the physical second coming of Christ. More than 2,500,000 copies of these books were circulated, and in all the large churches, a

55

sharp controversy developed between the Fundamentalists and the Modernists. It stirred the Methodist, the Episcopalian, and the Disciples churches, but it raged most violently in the Baptist and Presbyterian churches. The struggle began in 1916 and continues to the present day.

The people who made up the congregation that met in a rented store building during those early years were primarily from six local churches of different denominations, including Methodist, Presbyterian, Congregational, and Lutheran. It appears that doctrinal considerations figured largely in the formation of a new church organization.

The framers of the church constitution and statement of faith worked to create a church that would be independent of any denominational ties and faithful to the cardinal doctrines of Scripture as they understood them, particularly those under attack in liberal churches and seminaries at that time. Although its doctrine is essentially baptistic in character and its form of government congregational, the church has labored to maintain a flexibility in doctrine and practice that would enable people of diverse denominational backgrounds to fellowship together. Thus, such denominational distinctives as mode of baptism, Calvinism, or Arminianism have not been vigorously debated.

An institution must change or it will die. Numerous changes have been made in the ministry since it began. Its name changed twice before finally becoming Redeemer Community in the late 1950s. Numerous buildings and remodeling projects have resulted in a multipurpose building that is used to minister to Bible school children, boys' and girls' clubs, teenagers, and adults. The church has been characterized by capable pastoral leadership and sound topical biblical preaching. Its present ministry is the result of the cumulative ministries of effective and dedicated pastors. The most recent pastor served for sixteen years.

Four boards oversee the different areas of ministry: board of elders, board of trustees, board of Christian education, and an executive board, which is a combination of the previous three boards and the treasurers.

At the time of the consultation the membership was 343. The average Sunday morning service attendance was 265, 140 were at the Sunday evening service, and 73 in Wednesday evening prayer meeting. The average attendance for the year in Sunday School was 257. The average attendance one year earlier was 255.

The church has many "friends" who are not members but still give prayer and financial support.

THE PRECIPITATING FACTORS OF THE CHURCH CRISIS

A doctrinal crisis precipitated the crisis at Redeemer Community Church. Faith healing had been taught in some of the Sunday school classes in the church beginning about 1973. During that same year, an unstructured Bible school class was formed. The lessons were to be presented without prior preparation, only as the Holy Spirit directed within the class. During the same year, a number of the members of the church became involved in neighborhood meetings where the gifts of tongues, healing, prophecy, and exorcism were promoted. Most of those meetings were being held in homes and were led by visitors from other cities.

Healing meetings held in homes were attended by several members and friends of the church. At one of the meetings a significant healing was reported by one of the church members. That healing, reported early in 1973, precipitated a very positive reaction on the part of some and a very negative reaction on the part of others.

The growing unrest resulting from the promotion of the charismatic movement within the church membership was one factor leading to the pastor's resignation. The pastor's preaching had been sound theologically, but had been topical in form, leaving the constituency without an organized, Bible-oriented doctrinal foundation. As conflict developed over the nature of the ministry of the Holy Spirit, the members discovered that they did not have the biblical foundation to cope with what appeared to be false teaching. The pastor preached his final sermon on the ministry of the Holy Spirit and gave a strong exhortation to the church leaders to get some biblical teaching so that they might cope with the growing problem.

As soon as the pastor left, the promoters of the charismatic emphases felt they were now free to promote their position without hesitancy. Their promotion took many forms. Some began to be more involved in the music ministry of the church, whereas others began to share their teachings more frequently and openly in the Sunday school class discussions. One of the most disturbing features came at the close of each church service, when a few of the charismatically oriented individuals would invite others to charismatic meetings being held in the community. Some of the meetings being promoted were scheduled at the same time as regular church meetings.

The chairman of the board of elders at that point held an informal meeting in his home, to which he invited people both pro and con as far as the charismatic issue was concerned. The meeting gave him an opportunity to become better acquainted with what was actually going on both in the church and in the activities being held outside the church.

Shortly after that meeting, one of the church leaders made an abrupt change of position from noncharismatic to charismatic. That prompted a discussion at a supper meeting of the board of elders as to the need for clarifying the church's position on the matter. Seven days later, a special meeting of the board of elders was held, at which time they began to enter into formal discussion of the church's position.

After many meetings a statement on the work of the Holy Spirit, with special emphasis upon the gift of tongues, was prepared by the board. It was approved at the meeting of the board of elders and was read from the pulpit one week later. The restrictions emphasized in the statement were largely ignored by the charismatic group. It should be noted that the statement sought not only to clarify the position but also to outline restrictions related to matters included within the clarification. Among the restrictions was that of not allowing anyone to proselytize on behalf of any contrary position. The members of the church were also not to attend any meeting in which any contrary doctrine was espoused or promoted by the leaders of the meeting.

The members of the board of deacons and their wives instituted meetings with the leaders of the charismatic home fellowship. This was not only an attempt to keep in touch with what was happening, but it would also provide a chance to try to clarify some of the teachings of the group as far as Scripture was concerned. After two meetings, the group disbanded. There appeared to be no freedom for the Holy Spirit to work because there were some in the meetings who were not in accord with the neopentecostal position.

The charismatic group was invited to present their position before the board of elders. Shortly after the meeting was held, a demon or demons was reported to have been cast out of one of the children of one of the church members. This report increased the intensity of the movement and the division within the church over the issue.

Several meetings of the elders were held to continue discussions, evaluate the situation, and establish a procedure for possible remedy. Four paragraphs were formulated to attach to the original statement of the elders. The statement on the gift of tongues, with the four additional paragraphs, was distributed. The distribution of that document sparked a strong reaction. Negative feelings toward the statement and toward the elders who had formulated it were now at a high point.

By that time, one member of the board of elders, two members of the pulpit committee, the chairman and one member of the board of trustees, several members of the choir, and several in the congregation were more or less involved in the charismatic activities. After several more meetings, the board of elders realized that it could not cope with the problem. The only solution the elders could see at that point was the dismissal of some twenty-five members from the church roll.

The Point of Contact Between the Church and the Consultant

At their meeting in late summer, it was suggested that the elders call for outside guidance before taking that drastic step of disciplining twenty-five members. It was at that point that they called in the consultant. He made arrangements to meet with them at the church that evening. During the meeting which lasted several hours, he was made aware of the situation and was asked to serve as their church consultant.

A meeting was scheduled at which he was to present his understanding of the consultation arrangements and a general outline of the procedure to be followed.

At that later meeting, his report emphasized that the church should strive to maintain the same historical doctrinal position that it had held through the years. The same church polity should be followed, and the same characteristic features of the church's ministry should be continued. An emphasis was placed upon maintaining a stabilized ministry until a pastor would be called to provide needed leadership.

The church covenant, statement of faith, and church constitution would remain the same. The church would continue to maintain a Bible-centered, Christ-honoring pulpit ministry in order that the unsaved might have an opportunity to find Christ as Savior and the believers might receive biblical instruction for daily living. The church would maintain its independent nature as a non-denominational church. Organizations within the framework of the church and the church services would be guided by the doctrinal position and practices officially established by the church constituency. The consultant and leadership made clear that they were not opposed to change but that they did feel that changes should be approved by elected representatives of the church or by the church body at a regular church business meeting.

After making the points clear as noted in the preceding paragraph, the following two guidelines were established: First, the church consultant was to deal with all requests for changes in church practice. He was to discuss those matters with the proper church officials, and then he was to reply to the one making the suggestion regarding the disposition of the request. That reply would reflect the position of the church officials and the opinion of the church consultant. It would mean that there would be just one voice speaking publicly on church procedures and practice during the interim period. All complaints, suggestions, and requests from church members would be put in writing. They should be placed in a sealed envelope and marked "personal" for the church consultant. They could be mailed directly to him or left at the church office.

Now that the pastor had resigned and left, the responsibility for keeping the church in a stabilized condition fell upon the board of elders. It was really the first time that they had had responsibility placed upon them. They had little training and did not have the confidence of the church membership in general. The church at that point was ready to do what appeared right in each man's own eyes rather than that which would lend itself to general group stability.

The pastor had spent an excessive amount of time at the church and had done a great portion of the church work himself. He neither involved the lay men and women nor did he train them. He led the church in decision making. In fact, many decisions of rather major importance were decided without church consent. The church had developed a policy of disregarding the church boards, because the church knew that they really did not have the opportunity to provide leadership.

The second guideline pertained to a ministry of reconciliation. It seemed definitely unwise to force twenty-five people out of church membership until every attempt had been made to reconcile the people and positions involved. It was understood therefore that they would pursue a ministry that would strive to unite the body rather than divide it. Because of the second guideline, one of the members of the board resigned and severed his relationship with the church. He held such an antithetical position that there was no possible room for him to make even an attempt at reconciliation.

The next step was to establish some rather specific points of understanding regarding procedures.

1. The boards and committees of the church would not make policy decisions during the transitional period without discussing them with the church consultant prior to their adoption. This is imperative, since policy decisions can have far-reaching effects.
2. They would encourage the members of the church not to grieve or quench the Holy Spirit (Eph. 4:30; 1 Thess. 5:19) but rather walk in the Spirit and be filled with the Spirit (Gal. 5:16; Eph. 5:18).
3. The decisions of the board and the positions of the church during the transitional time would be communicated to the church body by the church consultant. There would be no surprises for the congregation to discover at a later time.
4. They would conduct the business meetings and make decisions as boards by majority decision and, whenever possible, by unanimous decision.

5. They would be open to receive suggestions for making the church services more helpful spiritually for all who attended. The suggestions would be considered by the church consultant and board and implemented as the Holy Spirit directed.
6. They would abide by the clarification of the doctrine of the Holy Spirit as formulated by the board of elders and circulated to the congregation.
7. They would insist upon the two following rules of practice:
   a. Glossolalia would not be advocated or practiced within church services conducted under the auspices of the church or within organizations that were considered part of the official ministry of that church.
   b. Since glossolalia is not a traditionally recognized practice within this church and its organizations, members of the fellowship would not use the church membership as an area for propagating the teaching pertaining to or practice of glossolalia. Members of the church would not be invited to meetings or be encouraged to attend such meetings by other members of the church. Members should not become open targets for propaganda of those promoting glossolalia. [It was the consultant's personal position that the end of section *b* overstepped the bounds of the legitimate control of the board of elders.]

The Problems Exposed and Procedures Followed During the Consultation

Near the beginning of the consultant's time with the church, he asked for permission to have an informal meeting with all of the people interested in the ministry of the church. He asked that the meeting be held on a Sunday afternoon for a definite time period of one hour and fifteen minutes. Permission was granted by the board. The board members were to serve light refreshments, wear name tags, refrain from giving public verbal answers to the oral questions that he would ask, and they were to take notes on the responses of the people. The substance of the responses, and not the names, was important.

Five assessment sheets, which appear in Appendix 2, were distributed, and the responses were later tabulated and reported to the people. They dealt with:

How I Feel About Our Worship Service

Church Finances

The Climate of the Church Organization

The Mission of the Church in this Community

Questionnaire on Congregational Purposes

The questionnaire on congregational purposes provided space for them to include what they considered to be the five outstanding purposes of a church. Those were collected and tabulated. They are included in Appendix 2-A.

When the questionnaires had been completed, the consultant asked the congregation to answer three questions:

What features of this church's program do you especially appreciate?

What features do you feel should be added to the church program?

What features should be changed in the church program?

One of the responses to the question pertaining to features that should be added to the program of the church mentioned the matter of a missionary conference. No one could remember when one had been held at that church, although the church had been interested in missions and had supported missions to a limited degree.

That seed, planted by one of the church members, took root in the minds of the people. The church held its first missionary conference one year later. It was extremely successful in every respect. They have now established it as a regular yearly function and make their plans a year in advance.

FINANCIAL CONFUSION

The financial situation at the church was another factor that encouraged the pastor to resign. Since there was limited involvement on the part of the people, the financial support gradually diminished. The pastor then turned to "friends" of the church for financial support rather than to the membership. Their support was often channeled toward provision for special projects instituted by the pastor without the full concurrence of the church. Two of those projects were the purchase of a new organ and the complete landscaping of the church grounds. When the projects began, the general treasury suffered, and a financial crisis developed.

In crisis consultation, churches very often have financial problems. When one part of the church is disturbed, that disturbance is often evidenced in the financial realm. That was true in Redeemer Community Church. The doctrinal disturbance and the deficiency in leadership contributed toward financial distress.

Redeemer Community had four treasurers and four accounts. Each treasurer was somewhat of a law unto himself. When the pastor was there, he kept an eye on the accounts. When more money was needed, he would often solicit funds from people outside of the church family to solve the financial dilemmas. That also meant he could do with the funds somewhat as he pleased, since he was largely instrumental in raising them. When he left, it took a little time for the financial difficulty to surface.

The laymen were now faced with the challenge of supervising the finances. They had not been trained, and they had not worried about them. The income began to decrease because of the instability evident to those who watched the leader leave with no one to take his place. Bills began to pour in, and there was not enough money to pay them. People began to demand bond payments, and there was not enough money in the bond balance.

By the time the consultant was called into the situation,

they had just mimeographed a list of the outstanding bills owed by the church and had circulated it among the members in hope that people would volunteer to go to the suppliers directly and pay the bills. The bills were from printing firms, hardware stores, utility companies, bookstores, and other organizations, and individuals. The church was also behind on the pastor's pension, secretary's pension, and money owed to the mission fund. The indebtedness in the general fund as of November 1974 was $4,432.39. The church had just taken out two $6,000 loans from the bank to pay for bond payments that had come due. The building fund indebtedness was about $122,000.00.

If one is to make constructive suggestions for the future, it is helpful to have some idea regarding the past. A survey of the past record took the consultant back to March 31, 1974, which was at that time the closing date of their fiscal year. The four church funds were in the following condition:

General Fund	
Miscellaneous bills	−$3,496.89
Christian education fund	− 1,935.85
Organizations and banquets	+ 7.68
Special (gifts and designated funds)	− 456.27
Organ Fund	
Receipts exceeded expenditures by	$4,082.76
Balance due to organ company	4,500.00
Unpaid pledges	682.00
Mission Fund	
Balance on hand	$3,359.11
Building Fund	
Balance on hand	$10,313.11
Total net indebtedness	122,744.89

The consultant then took a more telescopic view of the finances and summarized the church's accounts for 1971-72 and 1972-73. He compared those figures with the estimated expenses for 1973-74 and with what had actually been spent in 1973-74.

STATEMENT OF ESTIMATED EXPENSES
FOR 1974-75 FISCAL YEAR

	Spent 1971-72	Spent 1972-73	Estimated 1973-74	Spent 1973-74
General Fund:	$45,867.00	$ 53,316.00	$ 65,165.00	$ 60,005.69
Mission Fund:	24,884.94	26,119.10	27,244.00	27,423.45
Building Fund:	22,540.36	28,619.50	28,640.00	20,786.00
	$93,292.30	$108,054.60	$121,049.00	$108,215.14

Estimated 1974-75

General Fund:	$ 79,997.00
Mission Fund:	29,452.00
Building Fund:	29,630.00
	$139,079.00

The church had spent in 1973-74 a total of $108,215.14, which represented about $2,081 per week. They had budgeted for 1974-75 about $2,674 per week, but the average weekly offerings for 1973-74 had been only $1,975, $700 less than needed.

The next step taken was to establish a target date of January 1, 1975, in order to determine what the financial status would be at the present rate of expense and income.

PROJECTED STATUS TO JANUARY 1, 1975

General Fund

Present indebtedness	$ 4,432.39
Estimated expenses for Nov. and Dec.	12,000.00
	$16,432.39
	needed by Jan. 1, 1975
Accounts payable as of Nov. 10, 1974	$ 2,898.14

Mission Fund

No indebtedness as of Nov. 12, 1974	
Available funds	$ 894.71
On loan to general fund	500.00
	$1,394.71

Building Fund

Monthly payment due	$1,637.67
Deficit in bond reserve fund	6,003.28
Average weekly offering	275.49

 At this rate through May 1, 1975, there
 would be a total of $7,162.74.

Payments of the mortgage through May, plus loan and bond interest, would total $6,945.69. That would leave $217.05 toward bond retirement. *But,* the bond retirement schedule was to be around $5,000 to $6,000.

Conclusions

General Fund

Needed by January 1, 1975	$16,432,39
Estimated offerings for Nov. &	
Dec. at $1,300 per week	11,700.00
Anticipated deficit	$ 4,732.39

Mission Fund

Need during Nov. & Dec.	$ 4,000.00
Estimated for Nov. and Dec.	
@ $400 per week	3,600.00
Anticipated deficit	$ 400.00

Building Fund

Anticipated for Nov. & Dec. at	
average weekly offering of $275	$ 2,475.00
Nov. & Dec. payments due	1,099.34
	$1,376.34

The bond reserve fund deficit is now $6,003.28.

General Fund Offering	$1,300.00 per week
Mission Offering	400.00 per week
Building Fund	275.00 per week
	1,975.00 per week

(325 members, $6.08 each per week)

At this rate, we would have by January 1, 1975, a deficit of $5,132.39 in the General and Mission funds, plus the present Bond Fund deficit of $6,003.28, plus what is seen above the Building Fund Summary.

Several positive steps were taken to help rectify the

financial situation. The first was to share with the congregation some of the positive things that were happening. The people had lost touch with the church program. In November, an extensive report was made by the church leaders. The original copy that had been sent to the consultant was very long. It was not outlined and had extensive verbiage. The consultant felt the report should be outlined so that it could be more easily read. It should be on colored paper, so that it would attract attention, and it should be condensed so it would not take too long to read.

The next step was to supply *financial reports* to the congregation on a regular basis. The leaders could not wait for quarterly congregational meetings. The deficits were mounting too rapidly, and the congregation must be challenged to respond. Weekly reports were included in the Sunday service bulletins.

The board and consultant believed that it was imperative to assure the congregation that steps were going to be taken to *cut costs* so that the church would not find itself back in the same situation a few months down the road. Steps toward conservation were taken as listed below. The individuals immediately involved were notified, as well as the church in general.

1. Better telephone usage and control.
   Locks were to be placed on some of the telephones.
   Some telephone jacks were to be removed.
   A check was to be made of telephone rate programs.
2. Better light usage and control.
   Signs encouraging conservation were to be placed on the light switches.
   Persons were to be assigned to turn out the lights at night.
   Less light was to be used in the sanctuary and gymnasium.
   Locks were to be placed on the light switches in the Fellowship Hall.

Smaller light bulbs were to be used in several locations.

3. Weather stripping was to be placed on the windows.
4. Locked controls were to be placed over the thermostats.
5. The cost of the church paper was to be evaluated.
6. Consideration was to be given toward a percentage cutback of expenses for all departments.

Closely allied to cutting expenses was the *control of expenses*. The church board also took some definite steps in that direction. They authorized the formulation of a unified budget for a four-month period. Each segment of the budget was to have a budget controller. All financial information was to be made known to the church officers who were responsible for making purchases. Ordering was to be authorized by the proper person through a purchase-requisition system. Orders of over fifty dollars would require a second signature. They determined to employ a system for making a realistic estimate of expenses for the next year and to evaluate the figures after the first six months.

There were some areas in the present budget that could be cut. The pianist would no longer be employed as a paid staff member. No more music was to be purchased for the remaining portion of the church fiscal year. No more purchases were to be made for the church library. Literature purchases were cut. All extra social functions were curtailed unless provision had been made for them in the church budget. Love gifts, pay-as-you-go activities, and other functions that would "drain" the pocketbooks of the members should be curtailed unless approved by the church.

The ad hoc committee appointed by the church board made a report to the executive board in December. That report included five proposals, which were then accepted by the executive board. The finance committee then made a budget report to the congregation in January.

LEADERSHIP DEVELOPMENT

The third problem, beyond the doctrinal and financial, was that of leadership development. The former pastor had overlooked the matter completely. One of the important functions of a consultant is in the area of providing instruction and development of the leaders in order that they may enter more meaningfully into a truly democratic church procedure.

The consultant discovered near the beginning of his time with the church that the church leaders were willing to read materials and listen to tape recordings that would help them develop as leaders. The consultant served as a resource person in directing them to materials that would provide help. He shared with the leaders much of the mimeographed material that he had prepared for his seminary classes in church administration. They read the material and were able to correct former procedures and develop more constructive procedures. Many items pertaining to leadership training were added to the church library. Those were advertised in the church bulletin to provide help for future leaders.

A leadership seminar was held—the first in the history of the church—at the request of the board of deacons. It included the following agenda:

Session One: Breakfast
Session Two: "Goal Orientation and Leadership"
   Hymns
   Prayer
   Comments
   Consultation
Session Three: "Chat and Chew"
Session Four: "Organization and Job Descriptions"
   1. Election of officers: chairman, vice-chairman, secretary
   2. Appointments to special responsibilities: pulpit committee, nominating committee, finance committee, auditing committee

3. Establishing meeting schedules—time and place
4. Formulating purposes, goals, and objectives
5. Preparing a job description for each board member
6. Treasurers identify church purposes as reflected by the budget

   Analyze costs and formulate percentage diagram for the major areas of the budget

The seminar aimed at highlighting the importance of having goals and purposes for the church and the organizations within it. The new church officers had an opportunity to meet with the previous church officers and learn from them any helpful information they could share. The importance of job descriptions was emphasized, and the process of formulating them for all of the church officers was started at that point. The seminar sought to provide the leaders with an overall view of the total church program.

The church meetings had traditionally been upsetting experiences for the church. They had been poorly organized and poorly controlled. Now that the laymen were challenged to lead the meetings without the help of a pastor, and since there were very critical issues to be decided, they needed some guidance in the area of meeting management.

They learned how to construct printed agendas for such meetings and made them available to all present. The specific rules of order that pertained to each particular meeting were printed and distributed so that all in attendance would know the procedures to be followed. A competent parliamentarian was appointed by the board.

During the early part of the consultant's time with the church, he had discussed the matter of goals and purposes. That was also discussed at the leadership seminar and was presented in the mimeographed material circulated to the boards. He was interested in seeing the goals and objectives presented to the biannual business meeting of the church. They were presented and adopted. They had been formulated in response to quiet suggestions dropped by the consultant but were developed apart from any specific help provided by him.

BOARD RESPONSIBILITY AND ACCOUNTABILITY

The various boards and committees within the church had not been given responsibilities during the former pastorate. The pastor had either done the work himself or had made the decisions for the boards and committees. There were no job descriptions available. Just as there were no clear areas of responsibility, there were also no clear lines of accountability. The church was under a congregational form of church government in name only. The congregation did not exercise its power of control, so it was not important for them to receive or understand the reports of the boards and committees.

One of the first steps in correcting this problem was to publish the church constitution so that all could have a copy of it. It provided an outline of some of the responsibilities and some of the lines of accountability. As the boards and committees began to analyze those, they saw some of the deficiencies and some points where changes would have to be made.

Church constitutions from other churches were made available so that the boards and committees could compare their activities with those of other congregations.

Some confusion had developed in respect to the control of the staff members by the boards. The staff members were invited to the executive committee meetings as non-voting members. That gave the staff members an opportunity to become aware of the plans that were in process. It also gave an opportunity for the executive board to clarify areas of responsibility for the staff members. It improved not only organization but communication as well.

PULPIT COMMITTEE PROCEDURES

When the church consultant arrived, the pulpit committee had been in existence for about six months and had not really accomplished anything other than organizing. The chairman of the committee had been one of those involved in the doctrinal controversy. He was a strong proponent of the neopentecostal position. The lack of positive activity on the part of the pulpit committee had brought unrest to the congregation.

As the church began to realize that it did have some real authority and that it could and must exert it, pressure was placed upon the pulpit committee to act. The chairman resigned, and a new chairman was elected. None of the five members on the pulpit committee had served on such a committee previously. They were, however, very capable men and were ready and willing to learn. It was the consultant's responsibility to serve as a resource person for that committee. He met with them only three times during the entire period but made himself available for telephone calls from the chairman and provided printed material for all of the members.

The committee formulated a booklet, which was sent to the prospective candidates, that provided a survey of the church and community. They formulated a questionnaire that was also sent to the candidates and returned to the committee. Specific qualifications covering the expectation of the church on behalf of their new pastor were put into writing. Those were sent to each prospective candidate in order that he might prayerfully consider whether or not he would feel comfortable working in a church desiring that type of man. Regular reports of the activities of the committee were made to the congregation.

THE CLIMAX OF THE CONSULTATION EXPERIENCE

It is difficult in this church situation to pinpoint a particular climax as far as time is concerned. Results came in connection with each problem faced.

The doctrinal problem pertaining to the charismatic issue had been the conflict precipitating the crisis. The church's doctrinal statement of faith was clarified in statement by an 80 percent vote of the church at a specially called business meeting. That provided an objective basis for work in the future. One family left the church because of the board's adoption of a policy of reconciliation rather than that of excommunication of those holding to neopentecostalism. Two families that espoused the neopentecostal position left the fellowship of the church by choice.

The financial condition of the church was greatly improved. They adopted a unified budget so that they could be aware of the total ministry of the church. The three treasurers are now working together. The church is paying its bills as they come due. They have money in the bank. They have established a cash flowchart so their bond payments are scheduled in terms of their anticipated income. They have purchased and completely refinished a parsonage for their new pastor.

The church leaders, boards, and committees have assumed their responsibilities and are following the lines of accountability. The congregation is responding to the leadership of the church officers. Church attendance has been growing steadily. The Christian education program has had steady growth. One of the most phenomenal areas of growth has been in the area of visitation evangelism, which has developed without pastoral leadership. Visitation teams go out into the community each Tuesday evening. When the consultant last spoke at the church, nineteen young and older adults were received into the membership of the church.

The pulpit committee completed its work. A new pastor has been settled in the church and is living with his family in the newly acquired parsonage.

5

Garfield Memorial: Crisis in a Large Denominational Church

THE HISTORICAL AND GEOGRAPHICAL ORIENTATION OF THE CHURCH

The consultant first had contact with the Garfield Memorial Church in 1950. At that time they had had a medium-sized building with a fine, stable congregation. He had been teaching at a seminary in the area and served as a summer supply preacher. From that time until 1975, he had had no further contact.

A new building was constructed during those years. The old building was transformed into a gymnasium and Sunday school rooms. The new building increased the indebtedness of the church so that mortgage and interest payments amounted to about $28,000 a year. The building provided a beautiful sanctuary and more than enough rooms for the educational program. The thought at that time was that the building of a new church would serve to entice members of the community into the church.

The church had been affiliated for some years with a mainline denomination. In 1952, the church voted to sever its connection with that group and to seek membership in one more conservative. The change of membership was basically due to a theological problem. The original association was more liberal in theology than were the members of the church. A number of people within the church membership believed, however, that the church should never have changed its affiliation, a problem that kept coming to the surface during the years.

The Point of Contact Between the
Church and the Consultant

The consultant received a call from the assistant pastor of the Garfield Memorial Church. He was informed that they were without a pastor and was asked if he would be willing to supply the pulpit for five Sunday morning services. Their evening services were to be outdoor services held in the village park.

At the close of the first morning service, the assistant pastor approached the consultant on behalf of the church board and said that they requested a meeting with the consultant at the close of the second Sunday's morning worship service.

When he arrived at the study that Sunday, seventeen of the eighteen members of the church board had gathered. One led in prayer, and then they came immediately to the point of asking if the consultant would be willing to help the church during the time they were without a pastor. He made it clear that he was not available for the typical position of interim pastor, in which not only the Sunday preaching is covered but also the midweek services, weddings, funerals, and visitation.

The board had heard that he had served as a church consultant and asked if he would be willing to serve them in that capacity and do the Sunday pulpit work. His reply at that point was that he only took such work in churches where there were real problems. If they only wanted Sunday preaching and had no real problems, then they should get someone else, for he did not believe that such would be the place where God would have him serve. One of the board members, whom the consultant learned later was a sales representative and was gone almost as many Sundays as he was at home, spoke up and said that he did not think the church had any problems of great importance. A second member of the board spoke up immediately and said the board was divided "right down the middle" over the leaving of the last pastor and that it would still be divided when it came time to call another pastor. That statement in itself was enough to indicate some real problems in the church, although the number and extent of them were not known at that time.

The consultant asked for a week to give the matter careful and prayerful consideration. On the next Sunday, he told the board that he would be willing to help them, providing they and he could agree on procedures. At the close of his five Sundays of pulpit supply work, the consultant sent a letter to the chairman of the church board.

THE PRECIPITATING FACTORS LEADING TO THE CHURCH CRISIS

The chairman and eighteenth member of the board, who had been absent at the board meeting, was ill and passed away a few weeks later, not having had opportunity to resume his work at the church. The acting chairman was a professor and an educational consultant.

The consultant requested that he be given the month of July to study the entire situation. During that period, he held conferences with all staff members and read all of the church reports of the preceding ten years. He studied the Christian education reports and surveyed all of their financial records. He believed it was imperative to get the facts in the situation before making an attempt to help the church.

He suspected that there were many more factors behind his being requested to serve than merely to fill the pulpit during the absence of a pastor. Several of those factors began to surface during the month of quiet survey. Their extent would only be revealed during subsequent investigation.

In general consultation work, there is a tendency to work on solving one problem at a time, which involves some presuppositions. It assumes first of all that there is plenty of time. One can deal with the problems one by one until all have been handled. The second assumption is that one is quite sure of where to begin, which is a difficult position to take. Problem situations are complex. All that one can actually be sure of are the visible effects. The causes are usually not clear. Even if some of them are clear, they are several in number. In crisis consultation, the consultant has probably been called in from the outside, and there is no way to get the total picture in a short time. One must be thankful to find a number of the causes of the turmoil without presuming to expect to discover at once the major cause.

The consultant started to take steps to at least help rectify each of the problems that was evident. That type of approach has several advantages over that of the "single attack." In the single attack, one may miss the major problem. Here, one at least touches all visible problems. Another advantage is that many things begin to happen at once. That keeps the minds of the people so occupied that they do not have time to reflect upon the problems of the past. It sends many positive vibrations through the church so that practically everyone hears of some positive steps that are being taken. One can zero in later on problems that seem to need special treatment.

The board had requested that the pastor submit his resignation. That matter had brought a division within the board and ultimately a division within the church. When the pastor submitted his resignation, it included a stipulation that the church continue to pay him for six months. During that time, he would be relieved of all responsibilities and allowed to rest. The board was eager enough to have him leave that they accepted the stipulation and recommended that the church accept it. That brought more congregational unrest and board division. It also enlarged the financial problems of the church, which were already great.

Information was presented to the board, but they paid little attention to it and seemed to delight in becoming involved in rather meaningless motion. There was no written agenda and no prior notice of matters that might come before the board. Since the committees were inactive, the board became involved in dealing with minutiae that should have been the concern of committees. Therefore the board did not pay attention to the financial situation of the church or to the attendance statistics.

The quarterly meetings of the church were poorly attended. No committee reports were given, and no financial reports were given. There were no written agendas for the meetings, and there may not even have been unwritten agendas. As a result, neither the board nor church membership realized that at that time the church had a bank balance deficit of more than $3,000 and that the membership in the two Sunday services, midweek service, and Sunday school had gone down steadily for five years.

The staff had been notified that unless the financial picture was to be corrected, their salaries might have to be withheld. The treasurer had made inquiries regarding the possibility of refinancing the church mortgage. The interest rate would increase by about 3 percent, but the payments would be lower for the present. The utility companies were pressing the church for payment.

When the consultant arrived, there was no time to establish a long-range stewardship program. The people were not in the mood to have their "arms twisted" by a preacher asking for more money. The total picture had to be given to the board in a way that would catch their attention and to the church family so they might consider possible ways of meeting the crisis.

It was evident through their conversation, actions, and attitudes that interpersonal difficulties abounded within the board and congregation. The congregation was aware of the fact that there were problems because they saw the attendance decreasing in all areas of the church life and sensed the tension among the people. They did not know how serious the financial and other problems were. The church board was actually running the church, and the congregation did not receive reports of activities. They did get an annual financial report, but it was not easy to understand, and no time was given for any extended discussion. Communication between the board and the congregation was at a low ebb.

Members of the congregation had raised the question of denomination affiliation immediately after the exit of the former pastor. Some were saying the church had never really severed its connection with the original association and had not officially joined the second, conservative group. The question of denomination affiliation was heightened because the president of the conservative group was a member of the church, and the executive secretary of that denomination's foreign mission board was a member of the board of deacons.

With the decline in attendance and financial support, there was an evident lack of lay involvement in the church. The people were not responding to the call for service in the local church. It would be necessary to discover the reason for their lack of interest. The actual control of the church rested in the hands of only a few men, and women had been excluded from the work of the church to a large extent.

The Problems Exposed and Procedures Followed During the Consultation

GENERAL PROCEDURE FOR GENERAL PROBLEMS

The letter of acceptance sent to and accepted by the board was a very important document. It gave official permission to survey all church information. If that had not been made clear, the consultant would never have been able to get the needed facts.

The first responsibility listed in the letter concerned the administrative decisions that a regular pastor would normally make, including control of the material to be printed in the church bulletin. That bulletin became a channel of information immediately. The financial status of the church was dramatized so that the congregation could grasp the true situation. They saw, for instance, that they were committed to $27,700 of mortgage payments and interest each year. They saw that that exceeded their entire mission budget by $700. They became aware that they were more than $21,000 behind their budget up to that point in the year. It was made clear that they had a bank balance of minus $3,000. Projections were made indicating the length of time in which the trend could continue before the church would be bankrupt.

The giving of the church was noted in the bulletin and compared with the demands of the budget for each Sunday and with the offering of a year ago. The attendance figures with comparisons were also noted in the bulletin.

The congregation had not received that type of information in the past. They started going to the board members to ask that steps be taken to curtail expenses. Under pressure from the congregation the board placed locked shields over all of the thermostats in the church. The air conditioning unit was locked so that only the custodian could operate it. Two of the seven telephones within the church were removed, and one had a lock placed on it. Suppliers were notified that they should have purchase orders presented by those desiring to purchase and charge to the church. The insurance program for the church was reviewed and changed.

There had been somewhat of a running feud between the previous pastor and the choir. The consultant asked for permission to meet with the choir prior to his first Sunday service as church consultant. He assured them of his concern for their welfare and assured them of his support. He assured them that he needed their help and support, prayers and participation. Prior to that Sunday the consultant and his wife had sent corsages to the choir director and the organist, who were paid staff personnel.

He asked permission to have prayer with them before each morning and evening service, and continued the practice during his six months with the church. After about four months, the assistant pastor and he would take turns, depending upon the responsibilities at the designated time.

From the first Sunday, names were emphasized in the bulletin. That gave quiet but clear notice that the church leaders were interested in *people* before *program.* Students who were away at school, members who were ill, and individuals who were involved in the activities of the church were named in the bulletin.

The consultant gave notice near the beginning of his ministry that he wanted to have a special gathering for the senior saints. The invitation gave them something to anticipate and also assured them that he appreciated their presence and support. The program included a fine couple of senior adults from another church, who came with their accompanist and provided an excellent program of violin music. The assistant pastor had a travel slide presentation. Some special hymns were sung, which they especially appreciated. After the program, refreshments were served in an adjoining room that had been decorated in their honor. The response to that afternoon was refreshing and rewarding.

The consultant made available to board members an abundance of printed material dealing with church administration. They were encouraged to read it, but not pushed. They were thus given an opportunity to discover how to do things in the church without running the risk of "losing face" by having to ask someone for help. That material also helped stimulate some new ideas. One evidence of that was in the chairman of the board's formulation of a board manual. He had it printed and presented it to the board. It was the first time construction of such a manual had been attempted. The idea came from the consultant's printed material.

The pulpit committee had been elected prior to the consultant's contact with the church. They were inexperienced and seemed hesitant to seek help. The printed material circulated to the board and the new books placed in the church library provided them with the information they needed. They carried out their entire project with only one afternoon of consultation.

The fourth problem that demanded work was the problem of division within the church. Not only was the board divided, but the congregation as a whole was divided as well. The atmosphere was cold, and the people were not speaking to one another. One would really have to hunt in order to discover a smile.

A deacon was asked to develop a welcoming committee that would be at the door prior to every service. Two couples were appointed for each service. Name tags were provided, and their names were put in the bulletin each week. They were instructed to greet everyone, not only the visitors.

At the close of each service, the consultant would go to the rear of the sanctuary to shake hands with the people as they left. The assistant pastor stayed at the front of the sanctuary to help with inquirers. One of the members of the board of deacons was asked to stand at the opposite side of the door to greet people or to take notes from anyone with questions or suggestions referred to him.

The church gave advance notice when it sponsored after-service fellowship times. On some occasions a very short program would be presented, followed by refreshments, whereas at other times just singing, fellowship, and refreshments would fill the time. Name tags were used for the deacons and sometimes for other groups so that everyone could get to know the church personnel.

Another problem centered in the inaccessability of the pastor. His reports had emphasized how hard he had been working. But the people wondered how that could be, when they could not get to him to discuss matters. That was especially true when things were not running as smoothly as they should have been. There was no complaint department. If someone was unhappy, one could talk to everyone else in the church but not to the pastor. As a result, in many cases rumors and half-truths had spread like wildfire.

The consultant invited the board and some committees to meet with him, and they had a chance to see the study for the first time. They noted also that he had purchased and installed a coffee pot "with the trimmings" so that when people came to the study, they could have coffee with the pastor. Definite hours were publicized when persons could make appointments to discuss matters with him. In several cases, the consultant asked individuals to come to the study so that he could get to know them and discuss any matters related to the church that they wanted to discuss. He assured them that he would not be on the defensive and argue with them, but would rather give prayerful and careful consideration to any suggestions they might have. The staff members were invited to the study and knew that they could reach him at any time. He did not wait for them to be friendly, but took the initiative himself.

The letter of acceptance made provision for the consultant to have charge of the morning and evening services. Those services were important for many reasons. One of them was to set the tone for the church program. The worship services tell quite a story about the types of people who make up the church.

He changed the order of service in the morning worship to include lay participation. There was at least one layperson on the platform at each service. Opportunities were provided within the service for congregational participation. The morning service was formal, but not cold and stiff. The evening service was planned, but warm and informal. Hymns were selected to appeal to various age groups.

CHRONOLOGICAL OUTLINE OF SPECIFIC MEETINGS WITH THE CHURCH
BOARD AND CONGREGATION

First church board meeting. It would have been the
consultant's first choice without any question to make his
initial report to the church rather than just to the board.
He would have liked to have involved them from the very
beginning. But the situation seemed to demand another
procedure. The board and not the congregation was the
ruling body of the church. If he had insisted on going
directly to the church, he might have alienated the board.
It was also evident that the congregation had no experience in weighing and voting on decisions of conse-
quence. The church was actually too close to bankruptcy
to become involved in a process that would demand too
much time.

Although the men on the church board were actually
the ruling group, many of them were actually not acquainted with the facts. The board meetings were given to
transacting business that should have been dealt with by
committees.

The consultant became prescriptive to avoid having the
crisis come to a climax. He then worked toward cooperative consultation as fast as it seemed feasible. The consultant prepared a report for members of the board in printed
form and used it as a basis of discussion. Prior to the
distribution and discussion of that report, he circulated a
financial statement to the board. The format of the report
and the rationale for developing it are as follows:

CHURCH CONSULTANT'S REPORT

The Consultant Suggests That—
1. We not discuss past problems but concentrate on future possibilities.
   (The church had been split over issues connected
   with the last pastorate. There had been a general decline in all areas of the church life during the previous five years, and many in the church felt that some-

thing must be done. The pastor had been there for three of those five years. Realizing that things were crumbling, which was evident from his annual reports, he, together with a lawyer, made a proposal to the church for a sabbatical leave of six months. He would resign from the church, providing the church would accept that proposal.

That arrangement, with the events that led up to it, was instrumental in church attendance decrease and near financial collapse. The consultant's hope was to look to future possibilities and to keep the congregation so busy that they would not have time to discuss the unhappiness of the past.)

2. We give God the glory for all achievements and blame ourselves for the failures.

(This point was included because the people needed to recognize that the problem was a two-way street, and that possibly they should shoulder some of the blame for the desperate condition rather than shifting it all to the pastor.)

3. We recognize that this is not the time to change the foundations.

(1) No changes in the church constitution

(2) No changes in the church affiliation

(The situation was so unsteady that it seemed necessary to make certain there would be some unchanging foundations. If they started tampering with the church constitution, their energy would be expended at that point, and no forward progress would be gained. It would be a case of motion without real meaning.

There was a question in the minds of some regarding their denominational affiliation. The church board promised the congregation that they would investigate the matter. There was documented evidence that the church was affiliated with the conservative association. A few in the church did not want to accept that position and wanted the church to change its denominational status while they were without a pastor. The consultant believed that avenue must be avoided if at all possible. There is a time and place for all things, but he did not think that was the time to become involved in a denominational change.)

4. We use our own people whenever possible rather than hiring others.
   (1) To save money
   (2) To involve our people
   (3) To develop our people
   (The church had been trying to maintain an image beyond its means. As the statistics started downward, many drastic steps were taken to try to hold the line. One of those was to bring in expensive talent from outside the church family. The Sunday evening service became more of a showplace than a worship service. The church membership was filled with exceptionally fine talent that was not being used. They had dismissed the song leader and the organist, who had served for years without compensation, and had hired people from without the church family. The consultant believed they must either use their own people or lose them. They had already lost several.)

5. We emphasize participation in worship by our people rather than having them as spectators.

6. We have the morning service more formal than the evening service, but not stiff.

7. We have the evening service more informal as a praise service, but have it organized and planned.
   (The people in the congregation and especially the staff had become aware that the evening services had in many cases been planned on the spur of the moment.)

8. We spread responsibilities around so that when we lose one person everything does not collapse.
   (Their musical program had been centered in one professional musician, who had been imported. He had resigned the Sunday before the consultant arrived, leaving the church without a choir director, general music program director, or an organist. One man had served in all three capacities.)

9. We try to keep busy doing positive things so that there is little time left for negative considerations.

10. We emphasize a ministry of reconciliation.

11. We gather job descriptions for all staff, board members, and committee chairmen.
    (None of the staff members had job descriptions. Board meetings went from 7:30 to midnight and after because they were not sure just what they should be doing. The church committees were not meeting. Decisions were being made unilaterally by individual members since no one was quite sure of the responsibilities of the committees.)

12. We refer all complaints directly to the church consultant. That will free the board members to concentrate on constructive work.
    (The board members were trying to handle the complaints, which were numerous, from the church family. It became evident that they were not capable of handling them satisfactorily. They also would not have had the time, had they been doing the positive things that board members are normally expected to do.)

13. We encourage our people to suggest changes and improvements. Each one of those will be given careful and prayerful consideration.

14. We let it be known that we respect the opinions and

contributions of all of our people (men, women, and young people).

Seventeen specific suggestions were made in an attempt to be objective in the correction of some of the problems.

1. That an executive committee of the board be selected to work with the church consultant and pastor so that decisions can be made between meetings. These decisions will be reported at the next board meeting. Time is short. We cannot wait a month to make some decisions.

   (The church board met only once each month. Since there was only one board, all financial matters as well as other items had to be settled at that meeting, as the committees were not functioning. There were only four months in which to try to remedy the situation. It seemed imperative that someone work on the problems between monthly meetings. The consultant also needed some guidance regarding implications involved in some of the steps that might be taken. The previous pastor had requested this first item but had never succeeded in getting it passed. The board now voted to carry out this suggestion.)

2. That committees do their homework before each board meeting. They can then present their reports in writing and can as committees bring specific suggestions needing board action.

3. That the board and committees do not make policy decisions during the time of transition without first discussing the item with the church consultant.

4. That we include some specifics in the church bulletin:
   Weekly income
   Amount needed

Attendance at A.M., P.M., & S.S.
Prayer suggestions
   Serviceman of the week
   Shut-in of the week
   Student away at school
   Sunday school class and teacher
   Missionary Family
Status of mission budget
   and mortgage payments
   (once a month)

5. That the pastor and a deacon be at the door at the close of each service to greet the people.

6. That we have at least one man and one lady who will be ready to deal with inquirers who may indicate the need for spiritual help.

(People attending a conservative church like Garfield Memorial would expect invitations for commitment to be given at the close of most of the church sevices. But the church had not had an invitation given for five years, which was a cause for unrest for many. The consultant did not plan to give invitations at once but thought he should alert the people that they would be given in God's good time. That expectancy and hope served to quiet some of the unrest.)

7. That a deacon be on the platform at each service to help in the service.
Four men might rotate.
Each will meet with the pastors for prayer before the services.
   A.M. Extend welcome
      Conduct registration
      Give announcements
      (Possibly the prayer for the offering)
   P.M. Give announcements
      Call for the offering
      Give offertory prayer

8. That two couples serve as "Welcome Committee" at each A.M. and P.M. service. The names will be in the bulletin. They serve in the foyer of the church until the end of the organ prelude.

9. That we have two numbers of special music at each A.M. and P.M. service.

10. That we use both piano and organ at the A.M. and P.M. service. Have a regular organist but give our people a chance to share in the playing of the piano.

11. That we instruct the executive committee to divide our parish geographically so that each deacon can have the privilege of a "Watch Care" ministry over that zone.

    (The previous pastor had tried to get a visitation program started in which the deacons would participate. He had not succeeded for at least two reasons. The primary reason was that the deacons were not happy with the pastor and therefore hesitated to undergird the programs that he sponsored. The second reason was the lack of concern on the part of many of the board members for the general welfare of the congregation. There may have been a third obstruction— the board members' dread of hearing the dissatisfaction of the people on whom they would call. There was a need for a positive program of visitation. The consultant recognized that it could not be started at once, but the thought had to be planted.)

12. That we plan some informal fellowship times following the evening service.

13. That we plan for some specific ministry to the senior saints.

14. That we have either a regular or volunteer choir at each Sunday service.

15. That we institute a weekly prayer guide of a half page so that each prayer group will have copies.

16. That we send a letter to each missionary on our church missionary budget telling them of the arrangements during the transition period and assuring them of our support both in prayer and finances.

    (Whenever a church comes to a place of crisis, word spreads immediately. The missionaries who are on the field hear the reports and often fear for their own financial and prayer support. The reports that reach them are distorted. Letters were therefore sent to the missionaries in order to convey to them the facts and to assure them that the church would meet their needs. The church would hereby go on record as giving missionary support its top priority.)

17. That we take some definite steps to correct our financial situation.
    (1) Balance the budget by December 31
        Establish the amount needed per Sunday from September 1 to December 31 to meet our estimated actual needs.
        Take no offerings in the services except for budgetary needs.
        Emphasize stewardship in Sunday school and youth meetings.
        Take definite steps to cut down on utilities.
        Take on no new financial projects until after December 31.
    (2) Consider having missionary designated funds go toward meeting the budget of that item. If the designations are not enough, the church makes up the difference. If the designations exceed the budget sum, then all designations go to that project.
    (3) Designate budget controls for budget items.
    (4) Prepare a list of all outstanding bills (company, amount due, date).
    (5) Plan to arrange finances for next year so that it

will not be necessary to have a "crash" program at Harvest Home time.

(The church budget had been formulated without consideration of what they might expect to receive. There was almost no budget control. What there was stemmed from the action of one man. Any mission money designated to items included in the missionary budget went to the missionary, but it was not figured as going toward meeting the church missionary budget commitment for that missionary. There were many outstanding bills in the community, which, if left unpaid, would develop a poor image for the church in the community. In previous years, the Harvest Home offering that had originally been set up to help their mortgage payments had been used to meet their outstanding bills. It was a "crash" program each year.)

The final list of items for consideration were included in the report in order to let them realize some of the problem areas in the church beyond those with which we dealt in the previous notes:

1. Women's Missionary Society and/or missionary education
   (The Women's Missionary Society had disbanded during the last pastorate because they could not even get three ladies to serve as a nominating committee to propose officers for the coming year. That left the church with no organization to promote the cause of missions.)
2. Honoraria for musicians (music committee)
   (Due to the financial crisis, it would be necessary to terminate honoraria for musicians other than those employed by the music committee on a yearly basis.)
3. Stewardship committee activities
   (There was no stewardship education within the

church. Something must be done about that deficiency since income must be increased.)

4. A Sunday school directory
   (Sunday school attendance had gone down steadily
   for five years, as had the attendance at morning and
   evening services. The people needed to know which
   classes were available and where they were meeting.)

5. Visitation committee (calls each week on new
   people)
   (As new people would begin to attend the services,
   the church must be ready to follow up on this attendance.)

6. Decorations for church services
   (An excessive amount of money had been spent for
   flowers and general church decorations during the
   recent years. That was one place some money could
   be saved.)

7. Workers for Christian education committee
   (The Christian education committee found it impossible to get workers. There appeared to be three reasons
   for this; the general turmoil within the church body,
   the lack of information as to the needs, and the fact
   that the Christian education work was self-
   supporting. Since there was no financial support on
   the part of the church, the concern for its welfare was
   at a low ebb. One's concern often follows one's
   money.)

8. The pastor's revised job description
   (The assistant pastor had formerly been the youth director. When he was changed to the position of assistant pastor, he was not given a job description. Many
   still regarded him as only the youth director. Especially during this time of transition, it was necessary
   that there be a resident pastor at the church.)

9. Deacons will serve in their areas of strength and
   interest. Respect for individual differences.
   (It was quite evident that several of the eighteen board

members did not have capabilities matching some of the programs that had to be inaugurated. The consultant wanted them to feel that they could all do something, and that they would not be pushed into areas in which they did not have some competency.)

The consultant requested permission of the board of deacons to call an informal meeting of the church on a Sunday afternoon in September. He wanted to acquaint the church with what he was trying to accomplish.

Open congregational meeting. The notice of the meeting stated that refreshments would be served by the board of deacons and that the meeting would last for an hour and a half. It also stated that the consultant would be in charge of the meeting.

He asked that the board of deacons wear identification name tags since many of the church people did not even know the names of the deacons. They were also asked to take notes but to say nothing.

When the church members arrived, they were served refreshments—coffee, tea, or milk, and fancy cakes. They were welcomed at the door by the chairman of the board of deacons and the assistant pastor and their wives.

They were given five evaluation sheets, each printed on different colored paper. Pencils were provided, and the fact was emphasized that they should not include their names. The five evaluation sheets were titled:
- The Mission of the Church in This Community
- The Climate of the Church Organization
- How Do I Feel About Our Worship Service?
- Church Finances
- Questionnaire on Congregational Purposes*

The helpful information gleaned from the evaluations provided guidelines for future activity and methods of

*Lloyd M. Perry, *Getting the Church on Target* (Chicago: Moody, 1977), pp. 236-42.

procedure, and revealed the general status of some of the problem areas.

It was evident that the people of the church had a concern for the physical as well as the spiritual welfare of other people. They evidenced a desire to increase the ministry to the physical needs of the people in the community.

The climate of the church appeared to be quite good as one read the evaluation sheets. The consultant discovered, however, that those expressing negative attitudes toward the openness and friendliness of the church had very strong opinions. The consultant became aware that many of the very dissatisfied members did not attend the Sunday afternoon meeting at which the evaluation sheets were distributed. Those who did attend may have wanted to paint a good picture rather than face reality. He also learned that many who attended the meeting did not know what was actually going on within the church because of poor communication.

It was evident that changes could be made in the worship services without upsetting the congregation. It was also evident that they wanted some changes made. There was practically no dissatisfaction over the length of the services.

The church finance survey indicated that there was no strong feeling in favor of increasing missionary giving. It was evident that the congregation was not acquainted with the many segments of the church budget. The people were generally satisfied with the budget allocations.

Had the results of this survey been accepted, and the matter not pursued further, an inaccurate picture would have been drawn. Part of the reason for this statement is based upon the list of purposes they included at the bottom of the sheet. When those were carefully tabulated and analyzed, discrepancies appeared.

After the evaluation sheets had been completed, the

people were asked four questions. They were asked to respond informally to those questions, in order to obtain their forthright responses as a basis for future improvements in the church program.

- What do you especially appreciate about the program at this church?
- What do you feel are the outstanding weaknesses in the program at this church?
- What do you feel might be done to improve the program at this church?
- What comments can you share to help with the planning for the midweek prayer meeting?

The board of deacons kept a list of the responses to each question and tabulated those responses.

After the people had their refreshments, completed their evaluation sheets, and answered the four questions, the consultant read his report, which summarized his findings during the month of August and presented to the church the situation as it actually existed. It was the first time they had been shown actual statistics. The report shared with the church as a whole the report and decisions that had been accepted and passed by the board at its earlier meeting.

Second church board meeting. The next church board meeting was held only five days after the open church meeting. The following items were presented to the board in writing, and discussed extemporaneously. Interaction was encouraged.

1. *Some General Principles*
   a) Begin with purpose and then select materials and methods.
   The purposes of the church should be made clear to *all.*
   Each organization should have its purposes in writing.
   These should not contradict at any point the purposes of the church.

b) Involvement
   Use our people rather than lose our people.
   Have respect for all individuals and for individual differences.
   Work toward the day when no one will have two jobs until each has one.
   Avoid unilateral decisions.
   Have involved in decision-making the people who are involved in carrying out the decision.
   Solicit opinions (brainstorming sessions).
c) Communication
   Improve it between board and congregation.
   Improve it between board and staff.
   Improve it between board and pastor.
d) Organizational responsibility
   Draw organizational chart to show lines of responsibility.
e) Formulate job descriptions.
   Financial stability
   A realistic budget is necessary.
   Let the people know receipts and expenditures.
f) Let the people know the financial needs.
   Fellowship
   Hospitality and fellowship times for all ages.
   Welcome to Sunday school and church services.

2. *Some General Procedures*
   a) Ask specific people to do specific jobs.
   b) Make the constitution available for those who are interested.
      Do not contradict the constitution but be willing to plan in areas it does not cover
   c) If programs are not supported, be willing to let them drop.
   d) Have a written agenda for each board and committee meeting.
   e) If there is no business to transact, do not have a meeting.

f) Have each board and committee include a short report in the church bulletin after each meeting.

g) All meetings are to be conducted according to *Roberts' Rules of Order.*

h) Do the homework before each board or committee meeting. Bring in a proposal to be accepted, amended, or turned down rather than just discussing an area of interest.

i) Establish a starting and closing time for each board and committee meeting.

j) In a meeting, discuss motions, not discussions.

k) Have an executive committee of the board so that work can be carried on between board meetings.

l) Be willing to change and try some new approaches.

m) Emphasize the importance of trust, time, talk, and tolerance.

n) Be oriented toward the needs of people rather than the maintenance of an institution.

o) Have some training sessions for interested people dealing with church administration.

Third church board meeting. The next report was presented to the board of deacons at its October meeting. The report made the problems self-evident. It included two positive steps. The first was to have a budget that would include the Christian education program as a part of the church budget. The second step was to change the financial procedure so that money designated for missionaries included on the church missionary budget would go first toward meeting the church commitment for that missionary rather than bypassing the budget commitment. That report was later shared with the church family at its budget meeting.

The time had now arrived when the financial problem had to be faced, and some positive steps had to be taken to alleviate the financial strain directly. In preparation, the consultant mimeographed some information about church business methods and made it available for all of the board members. He purchased some copies of *Manual of Pastoral Problems and Procedures* (by Lloyd M. Perry and Edward J. Lias, [Grand Rapids: Baker, n.d.]) and suggested that the board members read the sections dealing with church finances. He had accumulated some comparative figures from the study of past financial records, mimeographed them, and distributed them to the board. A five-page brochure on General Principles for Church Work was also distributed to the board. The distribution of that material gave the board a chance to read and come forth with their own solutions or recommendations if they desired. It also provided good background support for proposals that the consultant would include in future reports.

Fourth church board meeting. In mid-November the next board meeting was held at the church. The leadership now had the financial figures available for October, so the consultant distributed a financial sheet that showed the trend from July through October. It also provided some budget comparisons.

If the church was to achieve the goal of having the church bills paid by December 31, it not only had to increase the income, but also had to take steps to control expenditures. Those steps had to concern the immediate situation and also make provision for the future.

THE CLIMAX OF THE CONSULTATION EXPERIENCE

The critical problem area in the church had been finances. Many factors had blended together to produce the crisis. The consultant believed that the aim should be to have all bills paid by December 31. That target date was not disclosed immediately with the people since it seemed too unreachable. But merely paying the bills would pose problems for the coming year. They had discovered that it was important to clear about $10,000 at the Harvest Home Festival so that an extra amount could be set aside to go toward the mortgage payments for the coming year. If the Harvest Home Festival money was taken to pay the immediate bills, they would be building toward another crisis.

Once the people became aware of the financial facts and aware of the December 31 target date, they began to work and pray toward that end. The Harvest Home Festival was held, and the offering on that one evening was $10,784.63. The church leaders now faced the challenge of paying all of the bills without touching the Harvest Home offering.

Expenses had been reduced, so the amount needed to pay the bills was also reduced. The church was obligated, however, to pay all actual bills, the missionary commitments, and the mortgage payments. The offerings the last Sunday in December totaled $5,305.30. There was still a need of more than $6,000 to meet the commitments. A regular watch night service was held on New Year's Eve. Some wonderful things had been happening in the church. Several had accepted Christ as personal Savior. Many had presented their lives to Christ for full-time Christian service. The spiritual warmth and friendliness of the church was very evident. When the offering was taken that night, received, and counted, the people had given $8,445.86. All of the expenses and commitments for the year had been met, and the more than $10,000 received at the Harvest Home Festival was available for the mortgage payments of the following year.

The people, in partnership with God, had brought to pass what had appeared to be impossible.

The entire climate of the church had been turned around in four months. The giving also continued in a positive fashion. This was not a one-time giving event but was just the beginning of a new giving pattern. During the first six months of the next year, the church giving exceeded the budget by $2,000.

6

Principles for
Church Crisis Consultation

Each church is like a person with a uniqueness, potential, and problems all its own. Each consultation does demand a certain special attention, but from a survey of various church crises situations, some general principles arise. You have read in the previous chapters the consultation experiences of one consultant in three churches that faced crises. The crises faced in those churches were in the area of administration, leadership, doctrine, and finances. The principles that have arisen from those situations are as follows:

1. Participate in the preaching ministry of the church during the consultation period.

That was the practice followed in all three consultation experiences. Preaching provides an opportunity for the consultant to lay spiritual foundations that are so important in the revitalization of any church. It provides an opportunity to deal indirectly with problems. The members of the congregation receive help and guidance from the preaching and then apply principles on their own. If someone other than the consultant is preaching, the preacher may be emphasizing points that are really not crucial at the moment. Preachers often become involved in answering questions that no one is asking. The consultant is aware of the problems and can make them central in his praying and in his proclamation of the Word.

105

The Holy Spirit speaks to people through the Word of God. We are dependent upon the ministry of the Holy Spirit as an essential factor in revitalization. The consultant therefore needs the help of biblical proclamation to support his work with God's family.

2. Establish and maintain solid communication links.

The use of the Sunday bulletin as a channel for information is important. This means that the consultant should ask for control of the information included in the bulletin. The bulletin should include a short report of each board and committee meeting held in the church. The congregation has a right to know what is happening. A weekly or monthly messenger can also assist in the dissemination of information.

Staff members should be permitted to attend board meetings. They do not have to vote, but they do have a right to know what is being planned.

There should at least be an exchange of minutes between the boards in the church. It would be better if one member of a board attended the meeting of the other board in the church. The pastor should attend board and committee meetings whenever possible in order that he be faced with no surprises when it may be too late to remedy a dangerous situation.

The congregation should be given opportunities to communicate with the church leaders. In all three churches, suggestion boxes were installed. Informal meetings were held with the members, and they were asked for their opinions. These opinions were mimeographed and made available to the entire membership. The slogan for consultation work should be No Secrets.

3. Recognize that the church should be an open system interacting with its environment.

That major system is composed of many subsystems linked to one another. It is impossible to tamper with one without affecting other parts of the system. There is a positive and negative aspect at this point. When a person works with one subsystem and does not realize that other subsystems will be affected, one may inadvertently create complex problems. From a positive point of view, when one makes well-planned moves in one area it may bring very positive results in other areas within the system. Definite evidences of this principle were seen in two of the three churches, in which finances were a problem. The financial deficiencies were made up, not by direct preaching, but by getting some of the other areas of the church life into a healthy condition.

4. Make certain that all reports can be understood.

Many church reports are not even read because they are too verbose. It is wise to avoid paragraphs wherever possible and to outline and indent the information. Dramatize the statistics, putting them in diagram and simple form so they can be grasped at a glance. Oral reports are not easily understood. When making reports to the church, put them in writing and distribute them to the people. Do the same thing at board meetings. Give the written reports in outline form, and verbally fill out the outline, allowing them to take notes on what is being presented.

5. Be a resource person for the church leaders, boards, and committees.

Do not become prescriptive, but be instructive. Provide a wealth and breadth of material, and let the people choose to adopt or leave according to their leading. That gives the leadership of the church an opportunity to be creative in selection. It gives them an opportunity to make proposals at a later date as though they had originated the ideas. The consultant should strive to be a king *maker* rather than a king. See the bibliography for a list of some of the reading material that was made available to the church leaders. Some also request that copies be placed in their church libraries.

6. Make wise use of your time.

You cannot do everything. Deal with the trouble spots

and the troublesome people. Find the "church boss" and help him or her to mature spiritually. When he is in favor of an item, many will follow his support. Get him to think positively toward what you are attempting to do with the help of the Spirit of God. In one church, two personal visits resulted in more than $11,000 being given to the work of the Lord in that church. God will guide the consultant toward meaningful areas of activity. Wait on the Lord! Set a time schedule, in your own mind at least, and work toward that point. Direct traveling saves energy and time.

7. Involve the laypeople in the work of the church.

One good place to begin is the worship service. In all three churches the consultant used at least one layman on the platform with the clergy. Use those laymen who feel that God has given them gifts in this area. Not all church leaders were encouraged to participate on the platform. Change the order of worship if necessary so that the parishioners have opportunities for participation. The format followed in those three churches included worship, hymns that were "singable" and meaningful, and unison Scripture printed in the order of service for the congregation to read before the receipt of the tithes and offerings. Instrumentalists beyond organ and piano were developed and used in all three churches. The choir made a meaningful contribution at every service. There was at least one number of special music besides the choir number in each service. Musicians within the church were used rather than importing musicians from other churches. Use your people or you will lose your people.

8. Be sure that you have the confidence of the people.

It is important that the consultant know how to get along with people. Interpersonal relationships are very important. Refreshments at board meetings were used to assist in this area. Sheets of humorous material from a business enterprise, distributed before the board meeting, often got the men smiling before the meeting started.

Work on starting and closing the board meetings on time. The wives of the members especially appreciate that. Also, refuse to accept a call to be a church consultant until the officials of the church have checked out your references.

9. Make use of both prescriptive and cooperative consultation.

The crisis consultant will begin with a heavier emphasis on prescriptive consultation than he would use in a regular consultation experience. The situation is critical, and some things must be done immediately. The people are not just concerned about having the ministry at the church improved; they recognize that it must be *saved*. In many cases they have tried to keep the wheels turning on their own and, having come to a critical point, are now discouraged. As soon as the very critical hours have passed, the consultant should proceed with cooperative consultation as far as possible.

10. Become acquainted with the church tradition.

The church is an open system interacting with its environment. History and environment do influence the total system. It is not wise to try to change traditions immediately. The consultant is a change agent and needs to know how to bring about change without disrupting the entire work. Even if you cannot bring about certain needed changes immediately, let the people know your intentions and implement them as soon as possible. Be faithful to your word.

11. Start working on what some might consider minor problems.

There really are no minor problems in church work. Each one can have far-reaching implications and ramifications. Some of the smaller problems are easier to work on than the larger ones. You can therefore get the people working on positive corrective measures at once. When they are busy, they will not have as much time to complain. As they see things happening, their enthusiasm will be stirred. Positive activity will bring motivation for more extensive work. Several examples of that principle were evidenced in all three consultations.

12. Be willing to invest some money.

A businessman knows that it takes money to make money. At Faith Chapel they were encouraged to spend money to restore fellowship between groups. The church had the money in the treasury, and in their case it was needed to restore fellowship. In another of the three churches the funds were so low that a Christian couple from another church made some anonymous gifts available so that a fellowship hour could be sponsored for the Senior Saints and fellowship times provided for the church as a whole. That church later began to take in more than $1,000 a month beyond its budgetary needs.

13. Take time to develop leaders.

Look for a few men with leadership potential and spend a great amount of time with them. Look for men that appear to have great leadership potential but need guidance and development. The church congregations in this study have noted the tremendous growth that has taken place in some of their laymen, who are now shouldering major responsibilities. That type of transformation does not take place by accident. It takes time and training.

14. Make clear that you have no "personal axe to grind."

The consultant should make clear from the beginning that he is not to be considered as a candidate for the church if it is without a pastor. He should make clear that once the consultation has been completed, he will not remain with the church. There is a time to come, and there is a time to go. The church consultant is somewhat of a "John the Baptist" who prepares the way for another who is to follow him.

15. Spend plenty of time obtaining the facts before making your move.

It is far more profitable to spend time in preparation

than it is to jump too quickly and have to spend an excessive amount of time in correction. Some problems will almost solve themselves when the facts are made public. This was true in the question of denominational affiliation that arose in Garfield Memorial Church. When the facts were made public, the former problem was no longer a problem.

16. Recognize the importance of financial accountability.

The people who support the church have a right to participate in the plans for spending that money. They also have a right to know that it is being carefully handled. They have a right to know that it is not being wasted. Uncontrolled spending of church funds will tend to short-circuit the giving.

ADMINISTRATION

Preachers have commonly had a very inadequate training in the area of administration. Courses in seminary may have been listed as having dealt with pastoral duties and church administration, but the actual course material has been weighted heavily in favor of pastoral duties. Confused administrative procedures in a church will often reflect the inadequate training some pastors have had. When a pastor is inadequately trained in this area, he might be wise to be willing to receive help from some of his laymen who are experienced and proficient in administrative procedure. The following suggestions were made to the churches involved in this project in the area of administrative procedure.

1. All individuals involved in changes must be notified before the changes are put into force.
2. It is important that the legal matters connected with the church organization be in proper order. This would involve such matters as the incorporation of the church as a nonprofit organization and the filing of the legal papers justifying tax exemptions and claims.

3. Keep a church record of and give public recognition for memorial gifts.
4. Emphasize encouragement during the time of a church crisis. Sharing of a list of accomplishments with the people of the church will increase giving.
5. Mimeograph and distribute the specific rules of order that are to control the church business meetings.
6. Invite staff members to attend board meetings as nonvoting attendants.
7. Help the people construct a step-by-step procedure for accomplishing what they are setting forth to do.
8. When there are individuals within the membership who are not happy with the ministry of the church, it is wise to deal with them personally rather than indirectly.
9. When there are doctrinal differences, think first of reconciliation rather than excommunication.
10. It is wise to have an understanding as to who is to be the one to speak officially for the church on controversial issues.
11. Manifest an interest in people of all ages rather than merely being interested in programs and problems.
12. Mimeograph and distribute thought-provoking questions that will stimulate boards and committees to discover facts and establish constructive procedures.

Meetings (Worship)

Church leaders and laity should gain proficiency in conducting various types of meetings. Those meetings would include services of worship, fellowship gatherings, and meetings for the transaction of church business. In the three consultation experiences included in this project, printed material was provided for the church leaders. The consultant also made the following suggestions:

1. It is important for the church to see the biblical basis and general purpose behind the elements in the order of worship.

2. It is important that people of all ages are given some social opportunities within the program of the church. At times those should be just for special age groups, such as the elderly, but at other times should involve all age groups together, such as at a church picnic.
3. Midweek services can be very important factors in the revitalization of a church. They provide time to clarify doctrinal points, impart biblical information, and establish a praying ministry.

LEADERSHIP AND TRAINING

Churches have been reticent to provide leadership training for the laity. There may be several reasons for that. Possibly the laity has been so involved in matters outside the church that they have no time for church leadership training. It may be that the pastors have thought that their own leadership position in the church would be threatened if the laity were to gain more proficiency in leadership. Whatever the reason behind the condition, laymen and laywomen in leadership positions in the church need training. The following suggestions were made to the churches included in this project:

1. Laymen and laywomen who have leadership positions in business enterprises cannot always make a satisfactory transition to leadership positions in a volunteer organization. Have the church leadership use and develop their spiritual gifts, but do not try to force them to do what they cannot do.
2. Leadership seminars should be held for the training of the laity. Laymen will be content only for a limited time to hold positions without responsibility or authority. They will finally rise up and demand a meaningful role. If that is not available, they will leave.
3. Low attendance at quarterly church business meetings may be indicative of the fact that they really have nothing meaningful to do in connection with the running of the church.

4. Be optimistic in your expectations. Expect great things from God.

FINANCES

The financial condition of a church often serves as a thermometer indicating the general and spiritual condition of the church as a whole. When members are dissatisfied, they will often withhold their giving, thus creating a financial crisis. Leadership problems will often appear in the confused recording and spending of church receipts. Inadequate planning on the part of the church will often be in evidence in the church's handling of bonds and financial commitments. The following observations were made to the three churches included in this project:

1. Extremely large financial givers will often expect to have more than their rightful share of control.
2. Restrict the taking of special offerings in the church services unless permission has been granted by the finance committee.
3. It is profitable to chart income and expenses. This pertains to the time past and to anticipation for the future. Portions of this chart should be shown to the entire congregation through the church bulletin or church newsletter. The entire chart should be made available so that the church leadership could note increases and decreases.
4. It is imperative that there be some financial controls. Cash flow and budget control charts are important.
5. Poor financial income in a church can be an indication of general dissatisfaction with the program of leadership.
6. It is wise to have an annual budget that gives the total church financial picture.
7. Financial support obtained from outside the local church constituency cannot be depended upon in times of church stress.

CONSULTATION PROCEDURE

It has only been in recent years that consultants have been used by churches. This particular project has dealt with churches in need of consultation from the outside as they faced situations that might well lead to the closing of the doors. Because of the dearth of printed material dealing with church consultation, and because of the very serious lack of guidelines in crisis consultation, the authors of this book have listed some observations that they found helpful.

1. Crisis consultation demands that you work on many problems at the same time. Your time is limited.
2. Crises do not come in a church because of just one problem. There may be one *major* problem, but there may also be contributing factors. There are no "insignificant" problems within a church.
3. If people are kept busy doing positive things, they will not have time or desire to meditate upon the negative matters.
4. It is important that the consultant be a resource person. Provide books and reading material so that those involved in changes can see the reasons behind the changes.
5. Stabilize what you have while working to meet the crisis.
6. Every consultation experience is unique. The consultant must be willing to adjust his plans in accordance with the situation that he faces.
7. The consultant must provide a supportive ministry to the church constituency. It is imperative that the church board and general membership have confidence in the consultant. In crisis consultation, the turbulence within the church makes it unwise to begin by trying to get the congregation to formulate goals. When the crisis has passed, then is the time to concentrate upon goal formulation. During the crisis, the goals of the consultant will have prominence.

8. A consultant should pay attention not only to the purposes and actions of the dominant culture of the church but also pay attention to the possibility of there being a latent culture with its own ways of doing things. Such a latent culture can rise to dominance.
9. It is wise for church leaders to seek outside help in matters where they do not have expertise. The matters pertaining to the charismatic issue at Redeemer Community Church needed the professional help of a theologian. That church eventually contacted a local seminary theologian.

COMMUNICATION

Many churches through the years have faced administrative crises due to a deficiency in communication among the leaders and between the leaders and the laity. The three crisis consultation experiences included in this project have highlighted the need for sharing information. The following suggestions were made to the churches:

1. When making changes, work through the proper boards, committees, and individuals.
2. Give notice ahead of time regarding encouraging events, thereby taking advantage of anticipation.
3. It is important that the people be given an opportunity to share their grievances. Pastors should listen to their lay people and sense their general areas of dissatisfaction. If those go unheeded for a long time, trouble is certain to come.
4. One effective way of settling unrest and dissatisfaction is to make all the facts available to all the people. Church bulletins are important channels of communication.
5. It is important to keep good lines of communication and good relationships among various age groups within the church.

7

Conclusion

Some years ago there lived in a remote area of East Africa a small primitive tribe of nomadic hunters known as the Ik. As survival pressures increased for them, they resorted to selfish, cruel, depraved, and deceitful actions beyond imagination.

Colin Turnbull of the American Museum of Natural History tells of the tribespeople's pushing their children out of the home to fend for themselves at age three, and exhibiting extreme cruelty to the elderly, the sick, and the injured. Survival of the fittest was for them the rule. Food was stolen from the weaker. The old and feeble became the objects of ridicule and targets for attack.

The elderly were sometimes pushed off cliffs for the amusement of other tribesmen and to reduce the number of mouths to feed. When a child was killed by a jungle animal there was great rejoicing since that indicated edible game in the area.

That incredible tribe gave up their fundamental humanity when the pressures on them via drought and governmental policies became critical. Although the extremes seen in the terrible disintegration of that primitive tribe are obviously not the problems we face in our local churches today, some principles can be derived from the situation that parallel our ministries. Pressures do come, and people do respond to them. The type and quality of response has been our concern in this book.

It should be recognized that all groups of human beings, whether tribes or churches, are going to undergo pressures from within and without. Our response to that pressure is critical. The Ik tribe turned in on itself and destroyed the tribe. That can happen in churches also, as people turn on one another rather than together seeking to solve problems.

If we would moniter our relationships, policies, procedures, climate of ministry, and factual data (financial, numerical, and the like), we would be in a better position to detect problems when they begin to arise, rather than go on opinion and feeling and let crises arise to the point where only drastic action will solve them.

We should be prepared for pressure-point breakdowns. Even the best equipment and the finest human organizations periodically need repair and revitalization. Having a strategy for meeting problems as they arise is one way of preventing major breakdown. Another and better way is to have a preventative maintenance program in operation. Having committees, boards, and other groups take the time to pray, play, plan, and produce through retreats, planning conferences, and other informal gatherings will help relationships develop properly.

We should seek and find help outside the group to assist in the problem solving and revitalization whenever problems arise that demand specialized help not available in the group or appropriate for a group member to undertake. Better still, seek guidance periodically to maintain the health of the organization.

This volume has been written to minister to pastors, boards of local churches, and leaders of Christian organizations of all types to provide direction and biblically-rooted guidelines in times of trouble. It is our prayer that it will also be of significant help to the church of Jesus Christ in preventing church and Christian organization crises.

Appendix 1

CHURCH SECRETARY JOB DESCRIPTION

Title: Church secretary

Employed by: The executive committee of the church board with confirmation by the church board.

Responsible to: The pastor

Termination of Employment: Two weeks notice by employed or employer or shorter time if mutually agreeable.

Rate of Pay: $_____ per hour up to 12 hours a week. If the pastor needs more time and the secretary is available, then a voucher for the additional time will be submitted and signed by the pastor.

Work Responsibility:
1. The work will be assigned only by the pastor. If the pastor is not available, the chairman of the board is responsible.
2. Work will include such items as:
   a. Type and print the bulletin each week.
   b. Answer the church telephone during assigned times of work.
   c. Establish an adequate filing system for church reports, Bible study materials, correspondence, etc.
   d. Care for the neatness and orderliness of the secre-

tary's office, conference room, and storage room.

e. Have charge of an office petty cash fund of $10.00. Keep record of expenditures and replenish the fund by turning in the list of expenses.

f. Make certain that there are adequate supplies. Check with the pastor, church chairman or treasurer, in that order, when materials such as paper are needed.

g. Type letters, reports for quarterly business meetings, etc., as assigned by the pastor.

h. Order plants, flowers, etc., from the church family for hospitals, funerals, or births.

i. Notify the appropriate person if the secretary is aware of some job that should be handled by some committee, but she is not to do their work herself.

Work Understanding:

1. Strict confidentiality will be maintained. This includes all matters overheard in the office or seen in incoming or outgoing correspondence. If asked for information by any of the church people, direct them to the pastor. Even when you are quite sure that certain things are to take place, refrain from telling anyone since nothing is certain until it has taken place.

2. When you have questions regarding the way things are being done, or when you may be less than happy with working conditions, types of work, etc., it is assumed that you will make that known to the pastor or board chairman. Otherwise we will assume that you are happy and contented.

3. Never hesitate to contact the pastor regarding any question you may have. When in doubt, by all means ask. The pastor will always have time to help you with your questions. If you make telephone calls from your home, keep a list, and you will be reimbursed.

4. The secretary will correct all spelling, capitalization,

and punctuation automatically without worrying about checking back. Wording will not be changed without permission except to correct the snytax.

5. The church will arrange for and pay the cost of a course at the telephone company for training in telephone technique. Your time and travel expense will be covered.

6. The Pastor's home telephone number and address are not to be given out except to people whom you know and in cases where for some special reason you cannot convey the message or contact him so that he can call the party.

7. The secretary will have keys to the church, secretary's office, and pastor's study. She will also have access to the key cabinet in which duplicates of all keys in the church are kept.

8. Do not hesitate to have prayer with people over the telephone, if they are in distress. Such spiritual ministries should be considered as having precedence over traditional office work. We are in a spiritual ministry.

9. Tell the pastor of all contacts that are made in the office. Share with the pastor other information regarding church matters that might help him make the Lord's work more effective. It is understood that the source of such information will be kept confidential by the pastor.

10. No Sunday work. This includes both the assigning and the doing of secretarial work.

11. Days are to be arranged between the pastor and secretary. Some kind of set schedule should be established—a minimal schedule. On any day the secretary is in the office six hours or more, she is to take a half hour lunch break. If her total hours per week exceed 12, she is to have the additional time

vouchered by the pastor.

Executive Committee of Church Board:

_____

_____

_____

_____

Secretary: _____

Pastor: _____

Appendix 2

2.A QUESTIONNAIRE ON CONGREGATIONAL PURPOSES

This is an instrument designed to help you describe your understanding of the purposes of this congregation. There are no right or wrong answers. Check the space that best expressed your perception. We are referring to the purposes in the church constitution.

1. The purposes of this congregation are clear to me.

   Agree 22 13 12 15 — 4 6 Disagree

2. The purposes of this congregation are merely implied.

   Agree 10 9 7 6 2 13 20 Disagree

3. Someone else has established the purposes of this congregation.

   Agree 18 7 5 7 4 3 22 Disagree

4. My personal purposes are consistent with the purposes of this congregation.

   Agree 17 11 19 10 2 3 5 Disagree

5. I have been involved in establishing the purposes of this congregation.

   Agree 19 6 7 6 2 9 20 Disagree

6. It is clear to me how we are moving to achieve our purposes.

   Agree 7 4 14 14 5 6 19 Disagree

7. The purposes of this congregation are unexamined by our present congregation.

Agree 18 5 8 11 4 7 14 Disagree

8. Our church program is planned in accordance with our purposes.

Agree 10 7 12 19 5 4 7 Disagree

9. Some parts of our program are not in accord with our purposes.

Agree 12 3 12 16 6 3 7 Disagree

10. List what you feel are the purposes of this congregation.

   1.

   2.

   3.

   4.

   5.

2.B HOW DO I FEEL ABOUT OUR WORSHIP SERVICE?

I think that:

1. The worship service reflects the desires of the total congregation.

Agree 13 10 12 8 8 7 12 Disagree

2. The worship service is regularly evaluated and reviewed.

Agree 17 7 7 5 6 10 13 Disagree

3. The worship service provides the kind of participation I want.

   Agree __27__ __22__ __3__ __6__ __3__ __2__ __10__ Disagree

4. There is flexibility and adaptability in the worship service.

   Agree __31__ __16__ __8__ __7__ __1__ __2__ __6__ Disagree

5. The hymns we sing reflect the preference of the congregation.

   Agree __22__ __13__ __12__ __11__ __2__ __4__ __7__ Disagree

6. The congregation has a sense of expectancy and anticipation.

   Agree __23__ __9__ __13__ __5__ __3__ __8__ __9__ Disagree

7. The sermon helps my worship of God.

   Agree __55__ __13__ __1__ __2__ — — — Disagree

8. There are elements in the worship service that need change.

   Agree __16__ __6__ __8__ __8__ __11__ __6__ __11__ Disagree

9. The length of the worship service is satisfactory.

   Agree __50__ __14__ __7__ __1__ — — __1__ Disagree

10. Change in the worship service upsets me.

    Agree __3__ — __3__ __9__ __6__ __6__ __46__ Disagree

11. There are some items in the worship service that should be omitted.

    Agree __9__ __4__ __4__ __14__ __6__ __6__ __28__ Disagree

2.C   CHURCH FINANCES

I think that:

1. Our church budget is too high for the number of con-
   tributors we have.

   Agree 16   9   7   7   6   6   20 Disagree

2. We should increase the percentage of our budget al-
   located for foreign missions.

   Agree 14   4   7   10   4   8   19 Disagree

3. Our church is doing a good job in stewardship education.

   Agree   8   2   5   12   8   13   19 Disagree

4. I am satisfied with the amount of financial information that the church provides to the membership.

   Agree 17   10   3   7   10   6   20 Disagree

5. There are some listed on our missionary budget
   whom I would hesitate to support financially.

   Agree   9   1   5   5   2   11   36 Disagree

6. Our church has a good financial reputation in the
   community.

   Agree 30   9   3   16   3   2   3 Disagree

7. I have a good knowledge of the amount and extent of
   coverage of our youth budget.

   Agree   9   5   6   9   2   7   31 Disagree

8. Our financial problems would be solved if we had
   more teaching and preaching on tithing.

   Agree   8   8   13   13   5   9   13 Disagree

9. More individuals and groups should be given a voice
   in establishing the budget.

   Agree 11   9   6   9   3   10   18 Disagree

10. I believe that our present budget allows for

	Too Much	Too Little	Enough	?
Music	2	7	41	15
Foreign Missions	3	20	29	11
Home Missions	3	21	25	10
Youth Activities	—	12	36	14
Heat & Light	6	5	39	11
Staff Salaries	3	13	37	10

2.D THE "CLIMATE" OF THE CHURCH (How It Feels Here)

We are interested in the overall "climate," or atmosphere, of this church. Although this is not a tangible thing, there is usually general agreement as to what the climate is, what it feels like at any given time.

The main point is this: how does it feel when you work with other people inside this particular church?

Check each pair of words or phrases below. Don't worry about whether you are precisely accurate, but give your best estimate of the "feel" of this organization.

THE CLIMATE OF THIS CHURCH ORGANIZATION

alert	15	14	16	13	5	5	4	not alert
mistrustful	2	3	2	9	15	16	19	trustful
cooperative	14	9	15	17	7	5	3	uncooperative
personal and close	13	15	14	10	7	7	7	impersonal and distant
creative	13	7	18	16	6	6	3	uncreative
insensitive	5	2	8	12	10	17	16	sensitive
facing problems	15	11	5	15	5	10	9	avoiding problems

conservative	12	10	14	19	10	3	3	innovative
unconcerned	5	5	4	9	8	24	16	concerned
listening	17	18	10	11	5	5	5	not listening
fearful	11	7	12	21	5	4	8	not fearful
rigid	7	5	7	14	14	11	11	flexible
feelings ignored	5	3	4	12	13	16	17	feelings count
divided	17	13	6	13	11	4	7	unified
relaxed	6	9	12	18	13	5	7	tense

2-E   THE MISSION OF THE CHURCH IN THIS COMMUNITY

I think that:

1. One of the major responsibilities of the church is to minister to the physical as well as to the spiritual needs of people.

   Agree __49__ __7__ __6__ __3__ __4__ __1__ __—__ Disagree

2. This church has clearly defined goals for its ministry to people in the community.

   Agree __8__ __5__ __10__ __14__ __6__ __8__ __16__ Disagree

3. This church is now as active in ministering to the physical and economic needs of people in the community as I would like for it to be.

   Agree __8__ __4__ __8__ __8__ __10__ __10__ __19__ Disagree

4. The church has an obligation to help its members minister to others in everyday life.

   Agree __50__ __10__ __5__ __1__ __1__ __—__ __2__ Disagree

5. The church ought not to get involved in controversial political issues.

   Agree <u>21</u> <u>7</u> <u>8</u> <u>10</u> <u>3</u> <u>3</u> <u>14</u> Disagree

6. The church ought not to get involved in controversial social issues.

   Agree <u>11</u> <u>6</u> <u>5</u> <u>11</u> <u>3</u> <u>10</u> <u>20</u> Disagree

7. I feel free to express to others in this church my views on controversial social and political issues, even though I know many persons disagree with me.

   Agree <u>19</u> <u>14</u> <u>7</u> <u>12</u> <u>2</u> <u>3</u> <u>11</u> Disagree

8. The minister ought not to take stands on issues even when he knows many disagree with him.

   Agree <u>9</u> <u>3</u> <u>—</u> <u>5</u> <u>7</u> <u>13</u> <u>32</u> Disagree

9. This church provides me ample opportunity of working with others in ministering to persons in the community.

   Agree <u>16</u> <u>9</u> <u>7</u> <u>13</u> <u>6</u> <u>8</u> <u>8</u> Disagree

Appendix 3

Academy of Management, Division of Management Consulting
Dr. R. A. Fosgren, Director of Membership
College of Business Administration
University of Maine
Orono, ME 04473

Institute of Management Consultants
347 Madison Avenue
New York, NY 10017

NTL/Learning Resources Corporation
7594 Eads Avenue
LaJolla, CA 92037

Organization Renewal, Inc./The Gordon Lippitt Group
5605 Lamar Road
Washington, DC 20016

University Associates, Inc.
7596 Eads Avenue
LaJolla, CA 92037

Bibliography

Academy of Management. "Proposed Code of Ethics." *Organization Development Division Newsletter*, Winter 1976.

Adams, Arthur Merrihew. *Pastoral Administration*. Philadelphia: Westminster, 1964.

Alexander, John. *Managing Our Work*. Downers Grove, Ill.: Inter-Varsity, 1972.

Argyris, C. "Explorations in Consulting-Client Relationships." *Human Organization* 20 (1961): 121-33.

Banet, A. G., Jr. "Consultation-Skills Inventory." In *The 1976 Annual Handbook for Group Facilitators*, edited by J. W. Pfeiffer and J. E. Jones. La Jolla, Calif.: University Associates, 1976.

Barnard, Chester. *The Functions of an Executive*. Cambridge, Mass.: Harvard, 1971.

Beal, George, et al. *Leadership and Dynamic Group Action*. Ames, Iowa: Iowa State U., 1962.

Beckhard, R. *The Leader Looks at the Consultative Process*. Rev. ed. Falls Church, Va.: Leadership Resources, 1971.

Bennis, Warren G. *Changing Organizations*. New York: McGraw, 1966.

————. *Organization Development: Its Nature, Origins and Prospects*. Reading, Mass.: Addison-Wesley, 1969.

Bennis, Warren G.; Benne, Kenneth D.; and Chin, Robert. *The Planning of Change*. New York: Holt, Rinehart & Winston, 1969.

Berne, Eric. *The Structure and Dynamics of Organizations and Groups*. New York: Grove, 1963.

Beveridge, W. E. *Managing the Church.* Cambridge: Allenson, 1971.

Blake, R. R., and Mouton, J. S. *Consultation.* Reading, Mass.: Addison-Wesley, 1976.

Blocsh, Donald. *Reform of the Church.* New ed. Grand Rapids: Eerdmans, 1970.

Bormann, Ernest, and Bormann, Nancy. *Effective Committies and Groups in the Church.* Minneapolis: Augsburg, 1974.

Brow, Robert. *The Church: An Organic Picture of Its Life and Mission.* Grand Rapids: Eerdmans, 1968.

Brown, Robert M. *Frontiers for the Church Today.* New York: Oxford U., 1973.

Buckley, Walter. *Sociology and Modern Systems Theory.* Englewood Cliffs, N.J.: Prentice-Hall, 1970.

Caplow, Theodore. *Principles of Organization.* New York: Harcourt, Brace & World, 1964.

Churchman, West C. *The Systems Approach.* New York: Dell, 1969.

Clark, Edward M.; Malconson, William L.; and Moulton, Warren, eds. *The Church Creative.* Nashville: Abingdon, 1967.

Daniel, James, and Dickson, Elaine, eds. *The Seventies: Opportunities for Your Church.* Nashville: Convention, 1969.

Dekom, A. K. *The Internal Consultant (Research Study 101).* New York: American Management Association, 1969.

Desportes, Elisa. *Congregations in Change.* Project Text Pattern Series. New York: Seabury, 1973.

Drucker, Peter F. *The Effective Executive.* New York: Harper & Row, 1967.

*Edge, Findley B. *Greening of the Church.* Waco, Tex.: Word, 1971

*Ernsberger, David J. *Reviving the Local Church.* Philadelphia: Fortress, 1969.

Etzioni, Amitai. *A Comparative Analysis of Complex Or-

ganization. New York: Free Press, 1971.

―――. *Modern Organization.* Englewood Cliffs, N.J.: Prentice-Hall, 1964.

Evely, Louis. *If the Church Is to Survive.* Translated by J. F. Bernard. New York: Doubleday, 1972.

*Fickett, Harold L. *Hope for Your Church: Ten Principles of Church Growth.* Glendale, Calif.: Gospel Light, Regal, 1972.

Fray, Harold. *Conflict and Change in the Church.* Philadelphia: Pilgrim, 1969.

Gamson, William A. *Power and Discontent.* Homewood, Ill.: Dorsey, 1968.

Gangel, Kenneth O. *Competent to Lead.* Chicago: Moody, 1974.

Geisinger, R. W. *To Revitalize the Church.* New York: Vantage, 1969.

*Getz, Gene A. *Sharpening the Focus of the Church.* Chicago: Moody, 1974.

Gibb, J. R., and Lippitt, R., eds. "Consulting with Groups and Organizations." *Journal of Social Issues* 15, no. 2 (1959).

*Gilkey, Langdon. *How the Church Can Minister to the World Without Losing Itself.* New York: Harper & Row, 1964.

Glasse, James D. *Putting It Together in the Parish.* Nashville: Abingdon, 1972.

*Gray, Robert N. *Church Business Administration.* Enid, Okla.: Phillips U., 1968.

Green, Hollis L. *Why Churches Die.* Minneapolis: Bethany Fellowship, 1972.

Havelock, R. D., and Havelock, M. C. *Training for Change Agents.* Ann Arbor, Mich.: Institute for Social Research, 1973.

*Hendrix, Olan. *Management for the Christian Worker.* Libertyville, Ill.: Quill, 1976.

Howard, Walden. *Groups That Work.* Grand Rapids: Zondervan, 1967.

Howard, Walden. *Nine Roads to Renewal*. Waco, Tex.: Word, 1967.

Johnson, B. C., ed. *Rebels in the Church*. Waco, Tex.: Word, 1971.

Jones, Stanley E. *The Reconstruction of the Church—On What Pattern?* Nashville: Abingdon, 1970.

Judson, Arnold S. *A Manager's Guide to Making Changes*. New York: Wiley, 1966.

*Kelley, Dean M. *Why Conservative Churches Are Growing*. New York: Harper & Row, 1972.

*Kilinski, Kenneth, and Wofford, Jerry. *Organization and Leadership in the Local Church*. Grand Rapids: Zondervan, 1973.

Kubr, M., ed. *Management Consulting: A Guide to the Profession*. Geneva: International Labour Office, 1976.

Kung, Hans. *Truthfulness: The Future of the Church*. New York: Sheed & Ward, 1968.

Kung, Hans, and Kasper, Walter, eds. *Polarization in the Church*. New York: Seabury, 1973.

Larson, Bruce, and Osborne, Ralph. *The Emerging Church*. Waco, Tex.: Word, 1970.

Lawless, David J. *Effective Management: Social Psychological Approach*. Englewood Cliffs, N. J.: Prentice-Hall, 1972.

*Lawrence, Paul, and Lorsch, Jay. *Developing Organizations: Diagnosis and Action*. Reading, Mass.: Addison-Wesley, 1969.

———. *Organization and Environment: Managing Differentiation and Integration*. Boston: Harvard, 1967.

Leas, Speed, and Kittlaus, Paul. *Church Fights: Managing Conflict in the Local Church*. Philadelphia: Westminster, 1937.

Levinson, Harry. *Organizational Diagnosis*. Cambridge, Mass.: Harvard, 1972.

Likert, Renis. *New Patterns of Management*. New York: McGraw-Hill, 1961.

*Lindgren, Alvin J. *Foundations for Purposeful Church*

Administration. Nashville: Abingdon, 1965.

Lippitt, Gordon L. *Organizational Renewal.* New York: Appleton-Century-Crofts, 1969.

Litwin, George, and Stringer, Robert, Jr. *Motivation and Organizational Climate.* Boston: Harvard, 1968.

McGavran, Donald A. *Church Growth & Group Conversion.* Pasadena, Calif.: William Carey Lib., 1973.

————. *Understanding Church Growth.* Grand Rapids: Eerdmans, 1970.

McGavran, Donald A., and Arn, Winifield C. *How to Grow a Church.* Glendale, Calif.: Gospel Light, Regal, 1973.

Mead, Loren B. *New Hope for Congregations.* New York: Seabury, 1972.

Mickey, Paul A., and Wilson, Robert L. *Conflict Resolution.* Nashville: Abingdon, 1973.

Paul, R. S. *The Church in Search of Its Self.* Grand Rapids: Eerdmans, 1972.

Perrow, Charles. *Organizational Analysis: A Sociological View.* Belmont, Calif.: Wadsworth, 1970.

*Perry, Lloyd M. *Getting the Church on Target.* Chicago: Moody, 1977.

Powell, Robert. *Managing Church Business Through Group Procedures.* Englewood Cliffs, N. J.: Prentice-Hall, 1964.

Reddin, W. J. *Effective Management by Objectives: The 3-D Method of MBO.* New York: McGraw-Hill, 1971.

*Richards, Lawrence O. *A New Face for the Church.* Grand Rapids: Zondervan, 1970.

Schaeffer, Francis A. *The Church at the End of the Twentieth Century.* Downers Grove, Ill.: Inter-Varsity, 1970.

Schaller, Lyle. *The Decision Makers.* Nashville: Abingdon, 1974.

————. *Hey, That's Our Church.* Nashville: Abingdon, 1975.

*————. *The Change Agent.* Nashville: Abingdon, 1972.

————. *Community Organization: Conflict and Reconciliation.* Nashville: Abingdon, 1966.

————. *Impact of the Future.* Nashville: Abingdon, 1969.

*————. *The Local Church Looks to the Future.* Nashville: Abingdon, 1968.

————. *Parish Planning.* Nashville: Abingdon, 1971.

Schaller, Lyle. *The Pastor and the People: Building a New Partnership for Effective Ministry.* Nashville: Abingdon, 1973.

Schein, Edgar. *Organizational Psychology.* 2d ed. Englewood Cliffs, N. J.: Prentice-Hall, 1972.

————. *Process Consultation: Its Role in Organization Development.* Reading, Mass.: Addison-Wesley, 1969.

Schindler-Rainman, Eva, and Lippitt, Ronald. *The Volunteer Community.* Washington, D. C.: Center for a Voluntary Society, 1971.

Schuller, David S. *Emerging Shapes of the Church.* St. Louis, Mo.: Concordia, 1967.

Seiler, John. *Systems Analysis in Organizational Behavior.* 3d ed. Homewood, Ill.: Irwin, 1967.

Smith, Clagett, ed. *Conflict Resolution: Contributions of Behavioral Sciences.* Notre Dame, Ind.: U. of Notre Dame, 1971.

Steele, F. *Consulting for Organizational Change.* Amherst, Mass.: U. of Mass., 1975.

Taguiri, Renato, and Litwin, George, eds. *Organizational Climate: Explorations of a Concept.* Boston: Harvard, 1968.

Tead, Ordway. *Administration: Its Purpose & Performance.* Tamden, Conn.: Shoestring, 1968.

Thielicke, Helmut. *The Trouble with the Church.* New York: Harper & Row, 1965.

Thomas, Donald F. *The Deacon in a Changing Church.* Valley Forge, Pa.: Judson, 1969.

Tucker, Michael R. *The Church That Dared to Change.* Wheaton, Ill.: Tyndale, 1975.

Vaughan, Benjamin N. *Structures for Renewal.* London: Mowbray, 1967.

Visser't Hooft, W. A. *The Renewal of the Church.*

Philadelphia: Westminster, 1956.

*Worley, Robert. *Change in the Church: A Source of Hope.* Philadelphia: Westminster, 1971.

————. *A Gathering of Strangers.* Philadelphia: Westminster, 1976.

*Especially recommended reading for church leaders.